GRAVEYARDS & CEMETERIES OF FIFE

CHARLOTTE GOLLEDGE

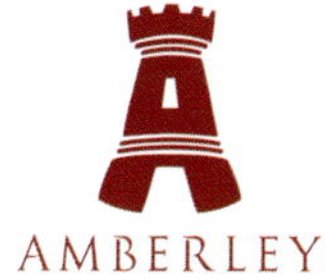

AMBERLEY

First published 2022

Amberley Publishing, The Hill, Stroud
Gloucestershire GL5 4EP

www.amberley-books.com

British Library Cataloguing in Publication Data.
A catalogue record for this book is available from the British Library.

ISBN 978 1 3981 1202 5 (print)
ISBN 978 1 3981 1203 2 (ebook)

Typesetting by SJmagic DESIGN SERVICES, India.
Printed in Great Britain.

Contents

Introduction

Few places are as deeply rooted in their history as the churchyard.

Thomas W. Laqueur

While this quote from Thomas W. Laqueur's book *The Work of the Dead* stipulates a churchyard, it applies to any burial ground, church/kirk graveyard or cemetery. It isn't always the stones or the people whose lives they commemorate, history is made in the events that take place there both past and present. The year 2020 will go down in many memories as one quite unlike any other in their lives. From minimal media coverage of a virus happening in other countries to a full-blown national lockdown in Britain that happened at an alarming speed.

Kingdom of the Dead.

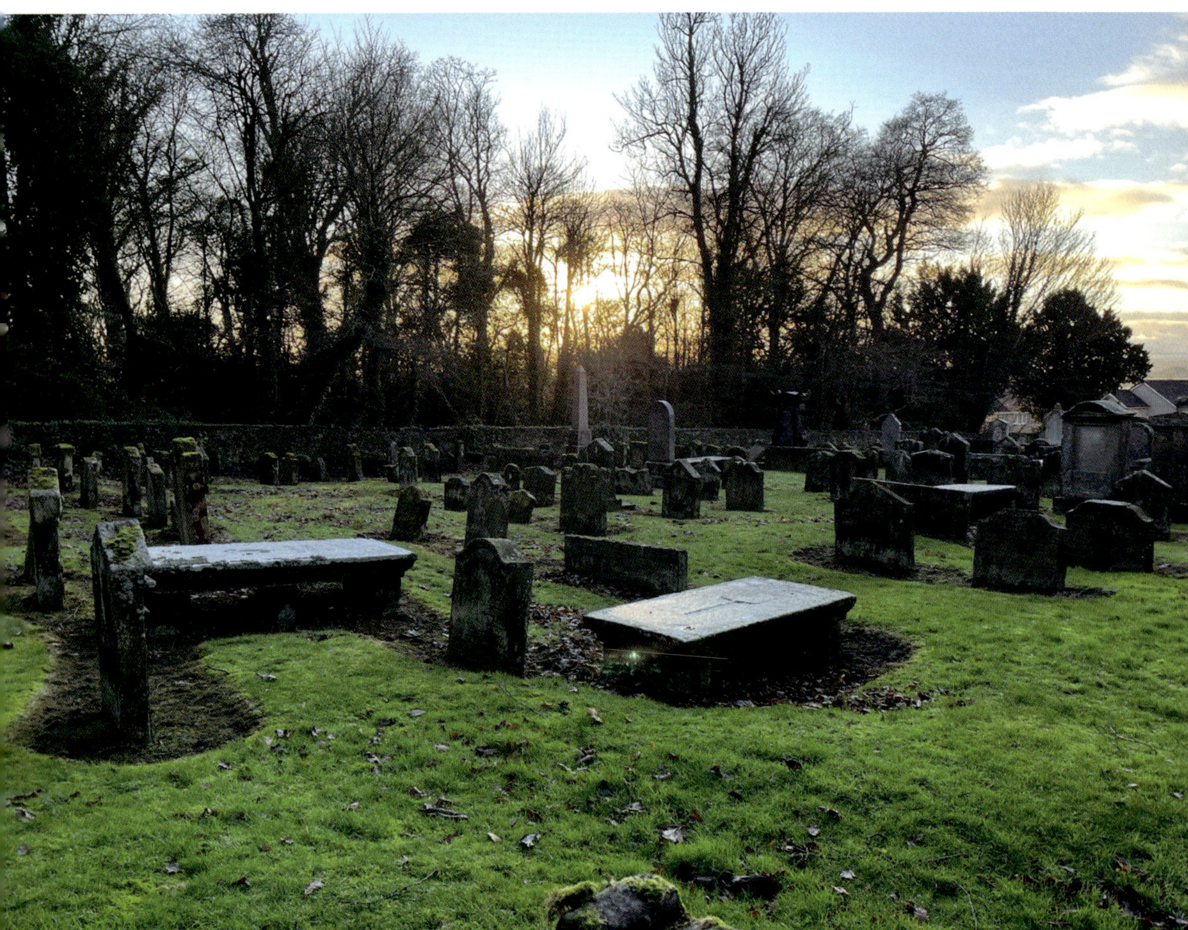

With entertainment venues closed, rules against visiting friends and relatives, and outdoor time restricted to exercise, green spaces became part of people's routines and a chance to pass a hello with someone who was not from your household. There was also a vast increase in the number of people visiting historic graveyards and with it a new-found interest in these peaceful spots and those who have long slumbered in the earth. Even as lockdown restrictions eased people were drawn back. I no longer found them a place for solitude. Instead, I took on the role of historian and entertainer when people's interests were piqued and the questions followed after watching my frantic scribbles and sketching, my nose up close to a carving from the eighteenth century.

While Edinburgh is famous worldwide for its magnificent burial grounds and being the final resting place for many great and esteemed people, as we move away from the capital, across the River Forth to Fife, we are plunged into earthier tales from all walks of life. For example, the burial place of ancient kings, queens and even a royal saint; the only witch's grave in Scotland; whispers of bodysnatchers scouring the kirkyards for fresh graves; or those who quietly lived their lives without any great fanfare. The grave markers left behind have drawn centuries of onlookers to wonder at all of their lives, for these are the tales of real people of Scotland told through their gravestones. Unfortunately, it is not possible to cover every graveyard and cemetery in Fife, nor even all the stories of the ones featured within these pages; therefore, there is a list of further historical burial locations at the end for you to explore at your leisure – be that in person or through the wonder of the internet. This book will also expand your knowledge of identifying the trades these people had in life from the symbology, which along with the funeral imagery and inscriptions, weaves an extra layer to their stories in stone.

Welcome to Fife's kingdom of the dead.

History of Fife

The history of Fife is long and saturated in mystery. It was one of the Pictish kingdoms and was known as 'Fib' up until 1165, when it was first recorded as Fife. The famous caves at Wemyss display markings dating from the Bronze Age, indicating just how long people have dwelled on this natural peninsula situated between the River Tay to the north and the River Forth to the south. Geographically set over 512 square miles and with the additions of both rail and road bridges to the north and south, many areas are now dwellings for those who commute to cities such as Edinburgh, Dundee, Perth and further for their employment. However, Fife's working past is steeped in home-grown trade, using its unique geography to its advantage.

James VI once described Fife as being a 'beggars' mantle, fringed with gold'. This description has been viewed two different ways: the first is the geographical description due to its frayed coastline of the mantle, with the begging hand held out to the sea in the hope of gaining sustenance from the bounty it brings; the

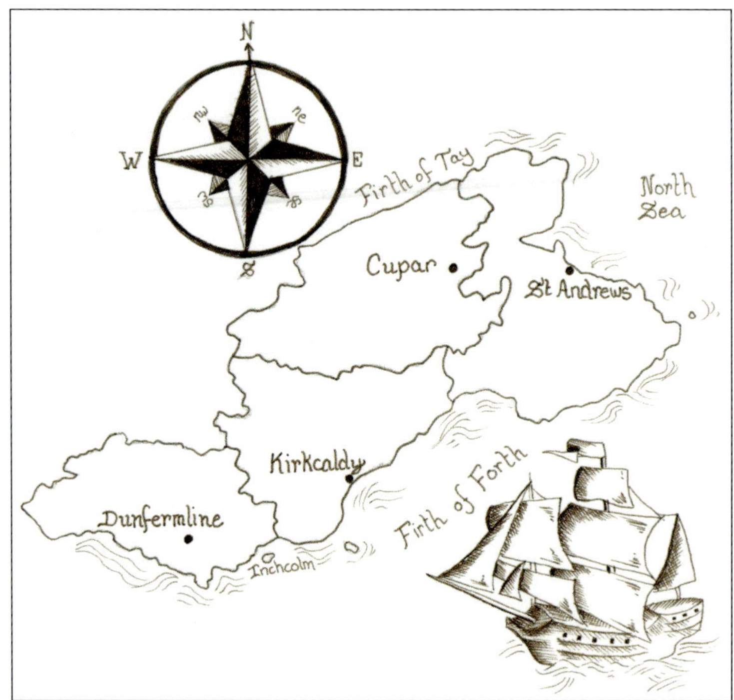

Map of Fife districts.

gold is the golden sands of the coastline. Meanwhile, economically it has also been considered that the king's meaning was due to the interior body of the land being thinly populated, while the coast, particularly along the Firth of Forth to the East Neuk, was populated with villages and royal burghs engaged in industries that generated wealth and commerce.

Based on the traditional presbyteries and for ease of travel, the county of Fife has been split into four districts – Dunfermline, Kirkcaldy, Cupar and St Andrews – generally going from south-west to north-east. There is also a separate section for the stand-alone burial site of Inchcolm Island.

Common Buildings in Fife Burial Grounds

Churchyards (or kirkyards) will have had a church building at some point, even if it is no longer evident due to it being demolished or converted into a mausoleum – a new church would then have been built elsewhere in the parish. There is also an increasing number of cases where a church building has been deconsecrated, sold and converted into a dwelling or such like. In most cases the grounds will still be under the ownership of the council and as such accessible to the public, though these should be visited in a way to cause the least disturbance to the residents. Churches, however, are not the only type of building to be found in Fife burial grounds…

Memorial Chapel

During the Victorian era a number of cemeteries across Scotland were created – burial grounds unattached to a parish. They were designed as great parks to commemorate the dead and were usually landscaped and adorned with trees and

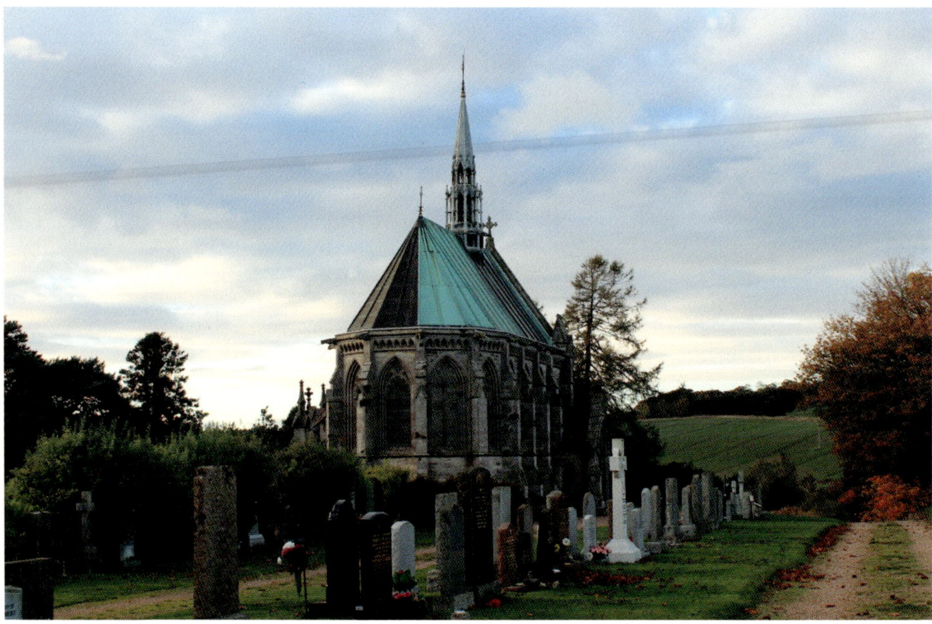

Vicarsford Memorial Chapel.

shrubs, designed to be inviting places to walk along the paths and contemplate those buried there. As such, they will not have a church building. There are a few rare exceptions in the form of memorial chapels, which are not intended as regular places of worship and as such are non-denominational. There is a particularly fine example at Vicarsford Cemetery, first dedicated to the memory of Lady Leng.

Watch House

The charter to the Guild of Surgeons and Barbers was awarded in 1505 where it was specified that they should dissect the body of one condemned criminal each year. This seemed acceptable for a time; however, eighteenth-century Scotland was witness to the establishment of the teaching of professional, apprentice-trained doctor surgeons. Edinburgh led the way with the College of Surgeons, appointing Robert Elliot on 29 August 1705 as its first Professor of Anatomy within the University of Edinburgh; Glasgow followed in 1720 with Thomas Brisbane; and the University of St Andrews appointed Thomas Simpson two years later. With these new schools came the need for bodies to learn the trade. It was said that every student needed three bodies each, and this was in addition to the bodies required for the public dissections that were undertaken by the teachers. In short, supply nowhere near met demand as the only bodies that were legally available were those of convicted criminals, whose sentence included dissection, and unclaimed bodies. Somewhere along the line those who needed bodies shifted their attention to local parish graveyards, and even those further afield.

The fear of the resurrectionist or bodysnatcher was deep-rooted for many in the eighteenth century and into the nineteenth, where this scourge reached its peak. Taking a body from the ground in this era was not against the law as it was technically not theft; only if a shroud or any belongings on the corpse were removed would it constitute a crime. While not illegal in the eyes of the law, the populace believed that apart from the moral wrongness of the act the flesh of the earthly body must be intact be able to rise and join the soul on the Day of Judgement. With life being so harsh for all but the rich, living a morally good life and cherishing the thought of a better place to go to when time in the mortal world was over was crucial to many. To make matters worse for the poor, the ideal body was one that was thin, emaciated even, as students preferred ones free from fat to work from.

The watch house was a purpose-built building either in the kirkyard or just outside its boundary walls. These buildings usually consisted of a single room with a fireplace. When a new burial took place the watch house was the shelter for those whose jobs it would be to keep the grave safe from the resurrectionists. It was not unheard of for men in this sort of trade to have informants within a parish who would send word when a death had occurred. Examples of watch houses still standing intact are at Abdie, Cairneyhill, Carnock, Culross Abbey, Kennoway, Kingskettle (converted into a private residence) and St Bridget's.

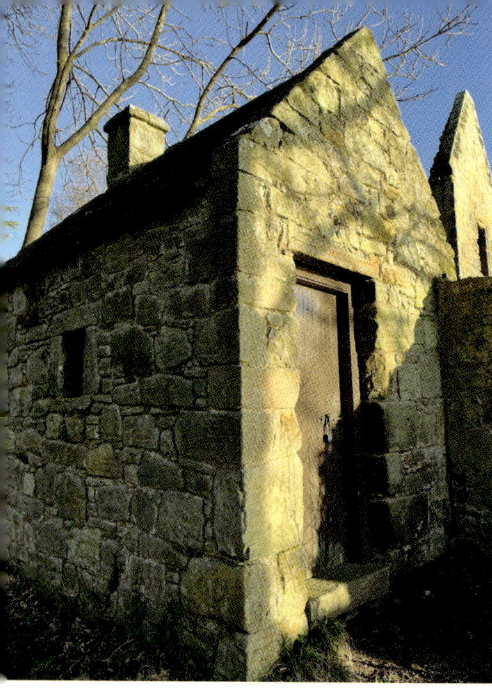

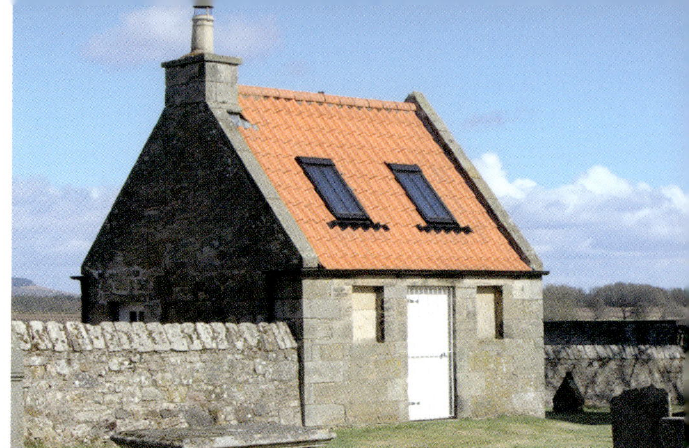

Above: Kettle Watch House.

Left: St Bridget's Watch House.

Mort Houses

There are three surviving examples of mort houses in Fife, at Abdie, Crail and Rosyth. They are all very different-looking buildings, but have one purpose in common: to protect the dead. They are solid buildings with tiny windows, if any, and have sturdy walls with a heavy wooden or metal door. The deceased would be stored inside the mort house for a specific period of time depending on the time of year and the season's air temperature. When it was deemed that the body would be unusable for the anatomists, the coffin and its inhabitant could be interred.

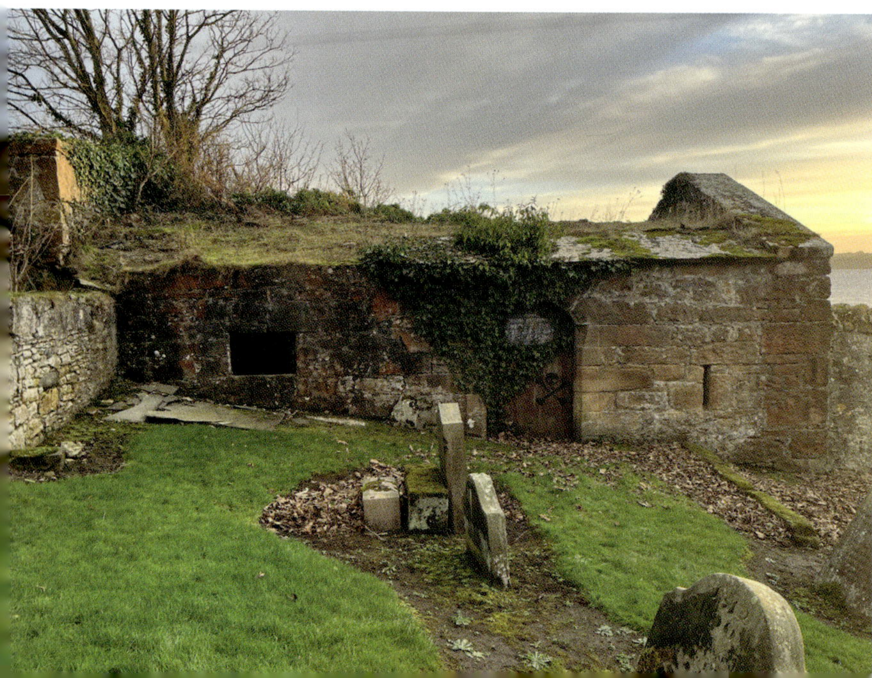

Old Rosyth Mort House.

Session House

The session house is a purpose-built building for the use of the parish kirk session, though some old watch houses were turned into session houses when their former use became redundant. The kirk sessions are local church courts that have been in operation since 1560 and the reform of the Church of Scotland. Comprised of the minister and the elders of a parish, the session's main duties were to maintain good order among the members of the congregation, which in the earlier centuries included the administering of discipline and ensuring proper moral and religious conduct as well as providing poor relief and education. The session clerk, usually a local solicitor or schoolmaster, was responsible for documenting the meetings, decisions, and transactions. While there was no set way a clerk would document parish life and the amount of information could vary between nearby parishes, session records remain one of the most valuable historical resources, giving a window into everyday life within quite a small local area.

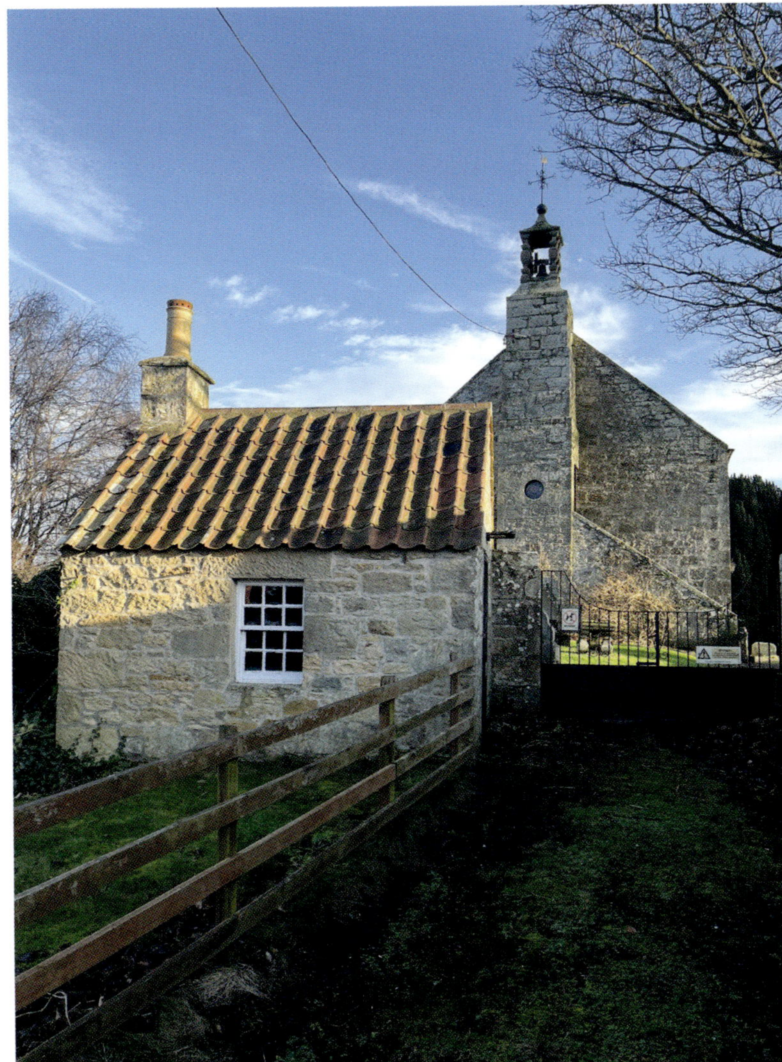

Kirkton of Cults Session House.

Tool Shed

In the nineteenth century many parish graveyards had their own tool sheds, often built from stone and designed in a way to be in keeping with existing structures. While many have disappeared some remain, though they are dilapidated such as the one at Monimal, which would have looked splendid in its heyday.

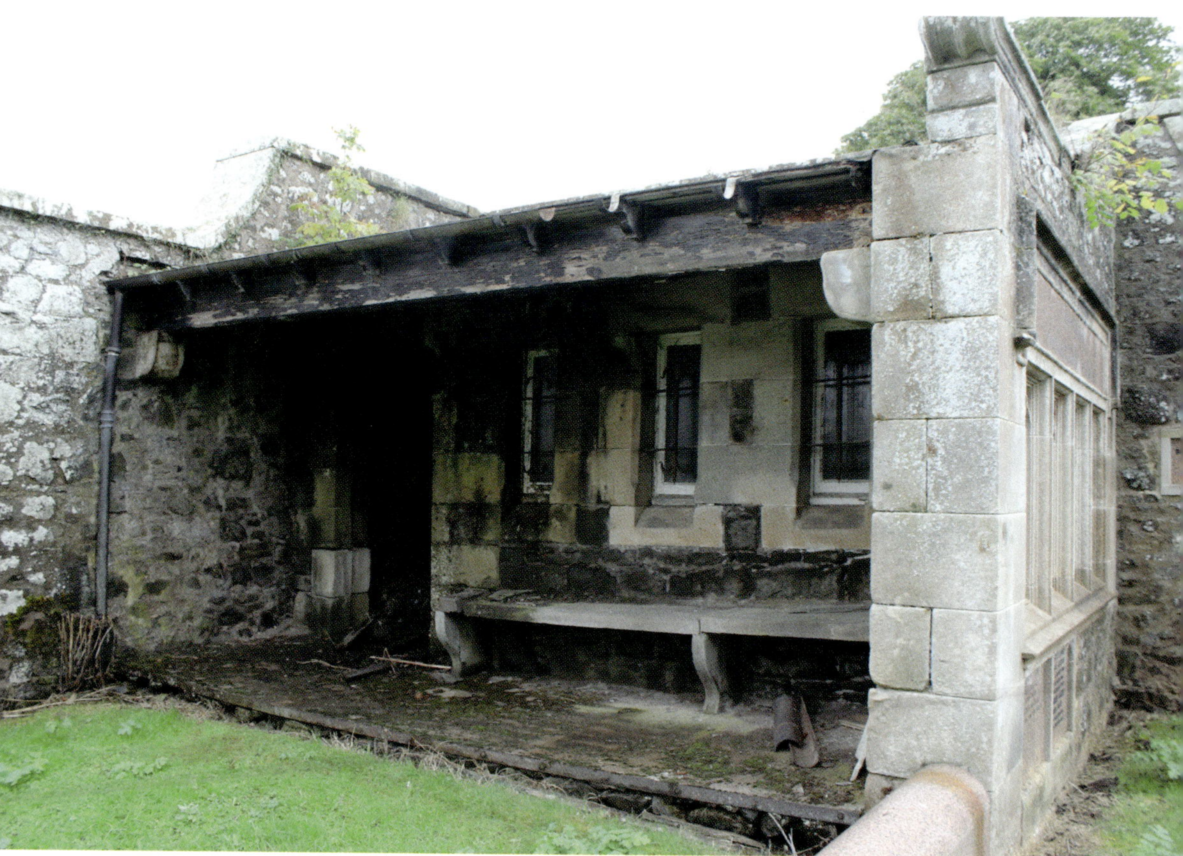

Monimal tool shed.

3

The Trades

Using the emblems of one's trade to decorate a grave was something the Romans would do. As with many Roman traditions, it is unsurprising that they made their way into other cultures even if centuries separated them. Right across Fife many of the graves from the seventeenth and eighteenth centuries will proudly display the trade its owner held in life, even if the name has long since worn away. It became especially popular after the Trade Incorporations had strengthened to such a degree that they provided financial protection for their members against merchants. In many churches the Incorporation Arms would be painted on the lofts where their members sat and upon their meeting houses and banners. In the rural areas a tradesperson (perhaps the only one of his kind in the small parishes) was seen as a figurehead – someone who could provide a skill needed by the whole community. It is perhaps why the great and noble have the most notable graves in Edinburgh's historic burial grounds, whereas in Fife the trades gravestones are more numerous.

Baxters

The baxters, or bakers, were one of the earliest trade communities to form in Scotland. Only a few of the baxters in a burgh would have ovens, leaving the remaining ones to pay a set fee to use them. They would regularly meet to discuss

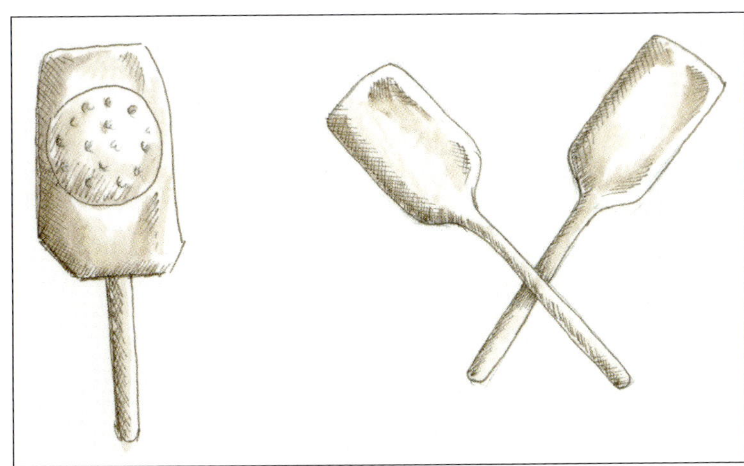

Baxter's peel with Bannock and crossed peels.

the buying and selling of grain; the quality, size and price of their produce; as well as discussing the ever-increasing concern that women were trying to enter the trade. Symbols include crossed peels, small loaves, bannocks, spurtles and scuffles.

Collier

Master colliers would have the pick and wedge on their graves. Sadly, coal miners of the seventeenth century were often shunned by others in society. In Culross they had to bury their dead outwith the parish graveyards. This changed by the eighteenth century, however.

Coopers

Coopers made a variety of wooden products, usually to hold liquids such as casks, buckets, barrels, troughs, etc. Journeymen coopers would also make wooden rakes and other such implements as they learned their trade. The most popular carvings are usually a cooper's hand adze, a type of tool that is used to rough out the end of staves; and a cooper's side axe, for chopping or listing barrel staves to a rough shape.

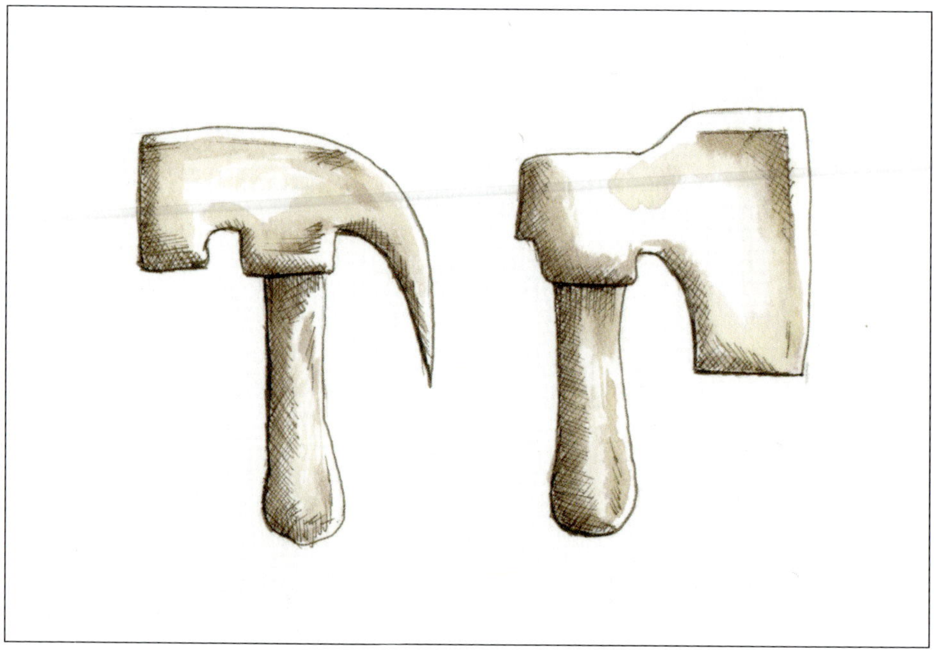

Cooper's adze and side axe.

Cordiners

The cordiners, or cordwainers, were traditionally craftsmen who worked with a Spanish goat's leather called cordovan; however the term evolved to mean 'a shoemaker'. The cordiners are one trade, along with the hammermen, to be allowed a crown. It is usually seen on memorials over the cordiner's knife due to a patent being bestowed upon them. Other symbols include the combination of pliers, sole cutters, awl, lasts or other cutting tools.

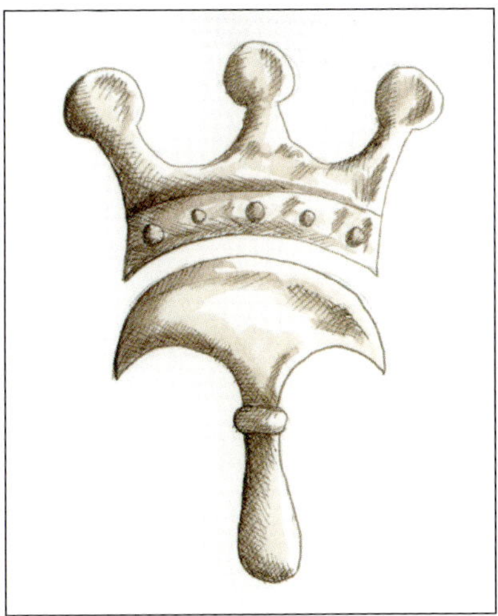

Cordiner's knife and crown.

Farmers

Given the geography of Fife, large areas were – and still are – dedicated to agriculture. The sock and coulter are the most common trade symbols to be found on graves, though they are sometimes also accompanied by the scythe, pitchfork, ox-yoke and butter churn.

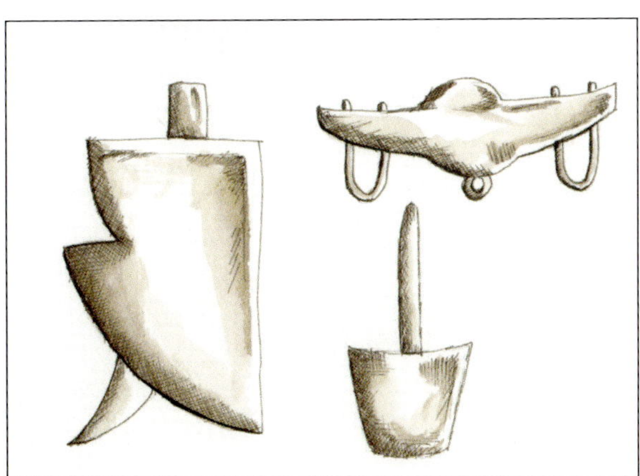

Sock and coulter; oxen yoke and butter churn.

Fleshers

Fleshers', or butchers', symbols are not hard to decipher. Most will include a flesher's knife, cleaver, axe and honing steel.

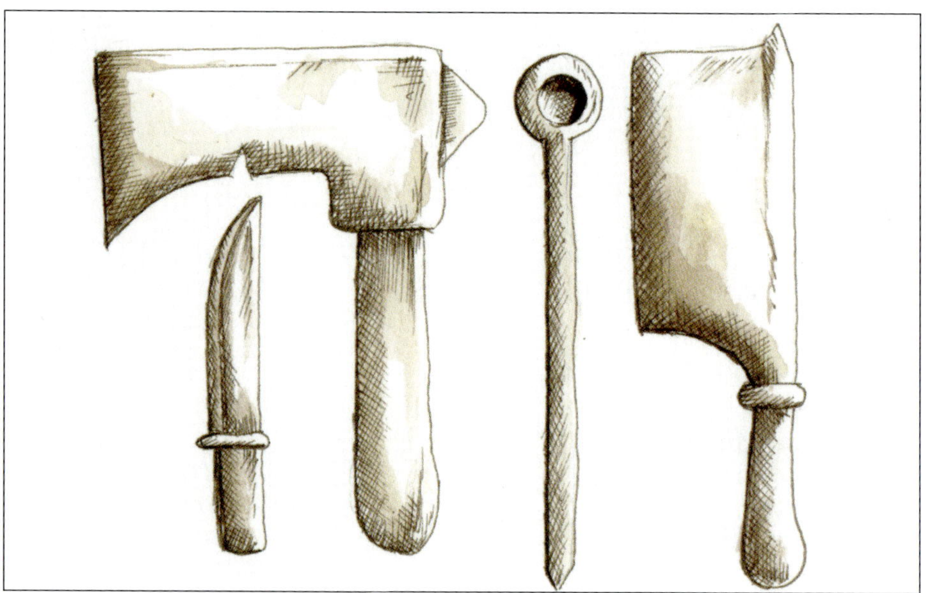

Flesher's knife, axe, honing steel and cleaver.

Gardeners

Gardeners were highly sought after by the wealthy, who wanted to have their gardens showcased as land cultivated for beautiful flowers and shrubs, and not solely for producing food. Symbols on gardener's stones are easily recognisable, though it is always a joy to come across the little-used watering can.

Hammermen

The Incorporation of Hammermen were granted the use of the royal crown on their coat of arms. However, those who were able to establish themselves as hammermen not only changed from era to era but also from place to place. Generally, the definition constituted of a craft that involved a hammer striking metal. The blacksmiths were without question integral to being part of the Incorporation of Hammermen – while still skilled labourers, they were held in a high social position. A blacksmith's grave will often include, along with a hammer and crown, a horseshoe or anvil, so there is no mistaking his trade in life. The craft also included armourers, culters, coppersmiths, griddlemakers,

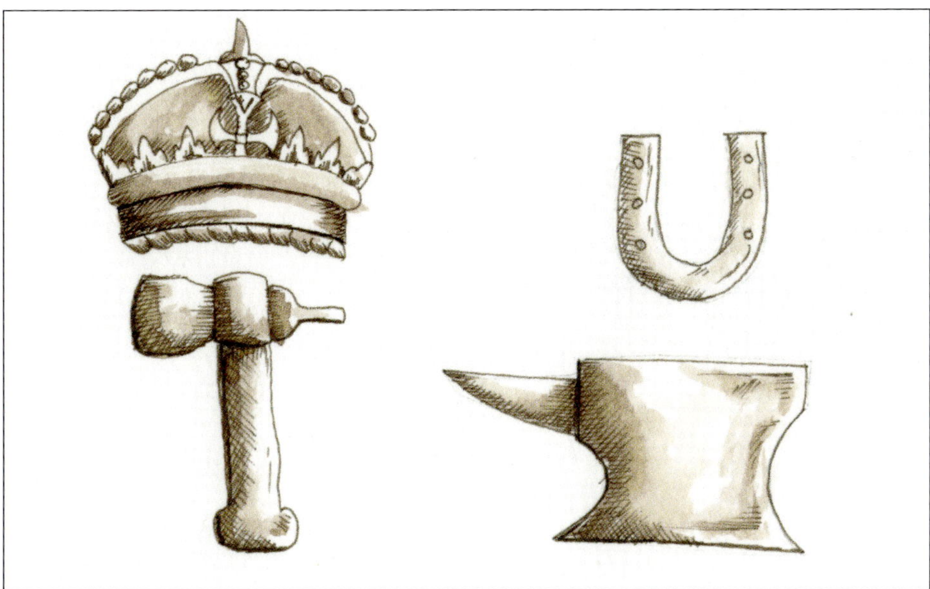

Crown and hammer of the hammermen, horse shoe and anvil.

glovers, goldsmiths, glaziers, hookmakers, pewterers, saddlers, tinsmiths, and watchmakers. This list is by no means exhaustive and so extra tools of the trade may need to be looked out for; however, often just the crown and hammer feature.

Maltmen and Brewers

Ale was a popular drink as it was a much safer option than water in many areas. By the seventeenth century maltmen were established in every town in Scotland and in most villages. The usual symbols to be found of their craft are the large

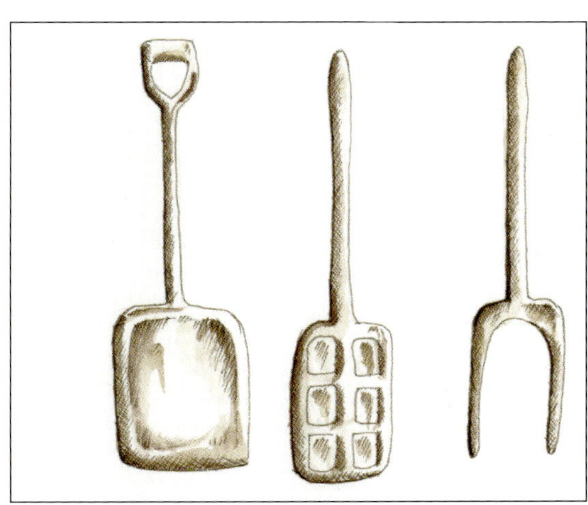

Malt shovels, mash oar and weedock.

malt shovels, tongs, mash oar or a weedock. If the grave belongs to a brewer, sheaves of corn or barley may be seen – sometimes accompanied by a barrel.

Mariners

Mariners cover a whole array of ship designs and navigational symbols, such as anchors, a compass, cross staff, and sextant. Rather than regional differences, mariners' graves can vary from one graveyard to another in a relatively short distance depending on the main type of sea trade or occupation held by the individual. The fouled anchor with its torn rope is for those who had served in the navy.

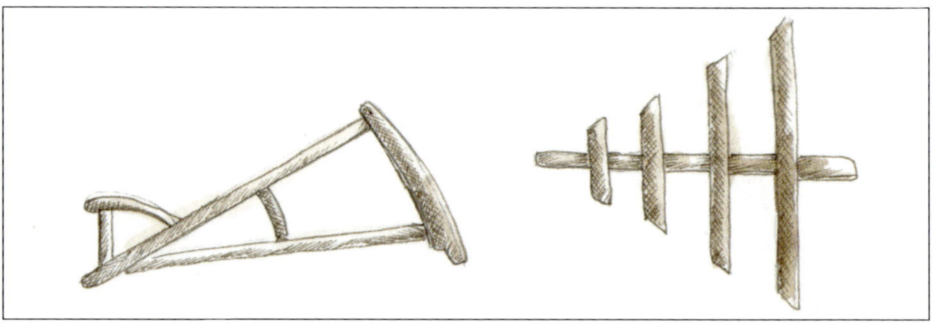

Above: Sextant and cross staff.

Left: Fouled anchor, Kilrenny.

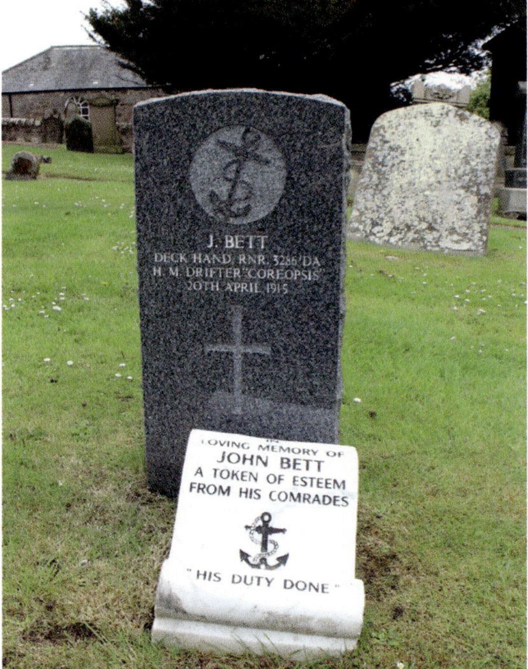

Masons

Symbols for masons include between one and three castles, a mallet, square and dividers, and a level and wedge. These should not be mistaken for graves of the Freemasons.

Ropemaker

So far there has only been one identified ropemakers' stone in Tulliallan. Being such an important shipbuilding area, it would be assumed there would have been more. The symbols are a short piece of rope and a rope spinner.

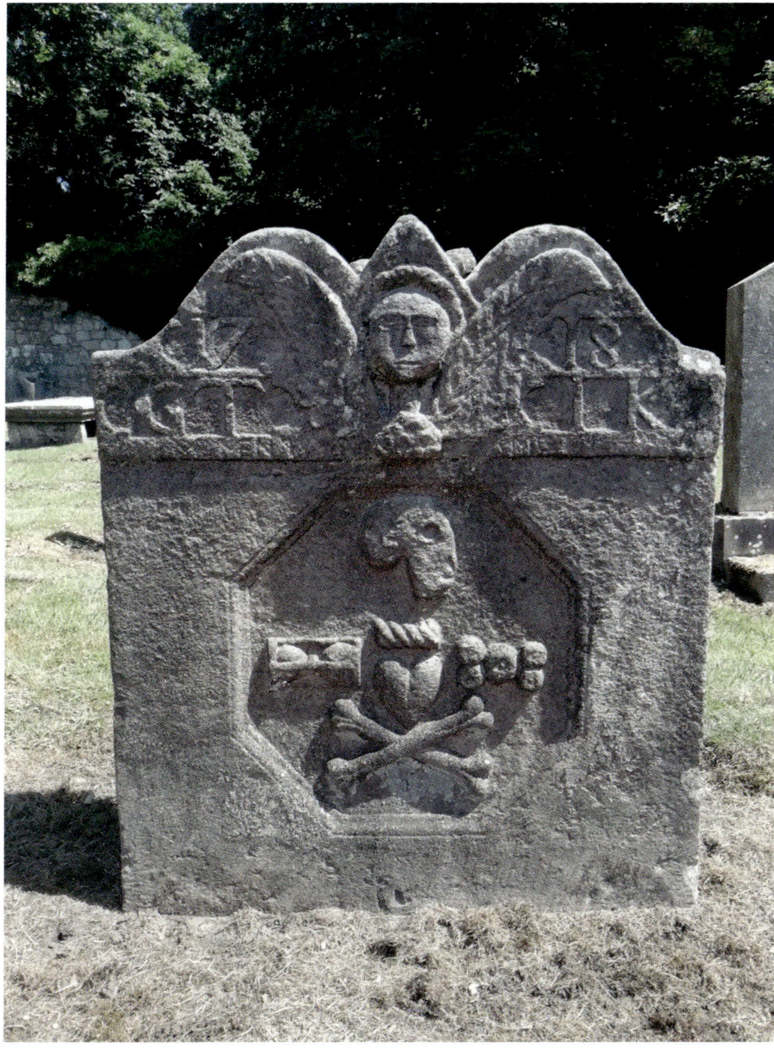

Ropemaker grave, Tulliallan.

Salter

The shovel and drawhook are tools associated with salters. These were essential pieces of equipment when producing salt in a process where it was evaporated from sea water.

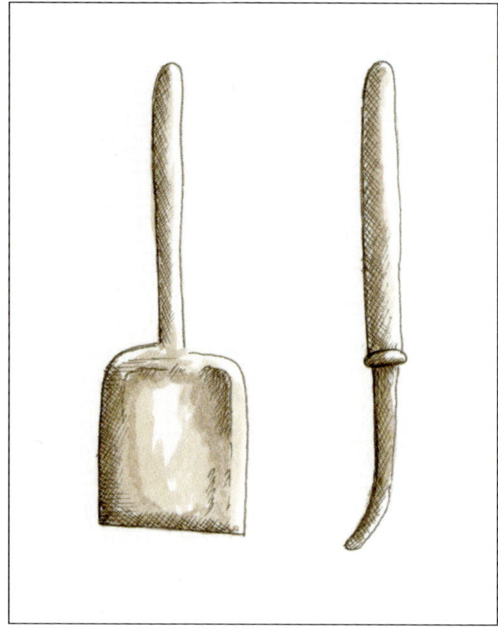

Salter shovel and drawhook.

Tailors

The Incorporation of Tailors was formed in Scotland in 1527. The most common symbol is the scissors and iron (either flat or goose), but a bobbin, needle, or the tent found on their incorporation insignia may also be found. The skill of a tailor could bring him great wealth.

Weavers

Great areas of Fife, especially in the northern rural communities, undertook weaving, although considering the number of weavers there are relatively few weavers' stones. An assumption drawn from this could be that only master weavers made enough of a profit to have a stone befitting them. This is further backed by the sporadic appearance of a leopard with a shuttle in its mouth, part of the crest of the Incorporation of Weavers, which had so far been identified at Kennoway, Ceres and Falkland. Weavers' stones predominately feature the shuttle, which is sometimes accompanied by stretchers and card combs.

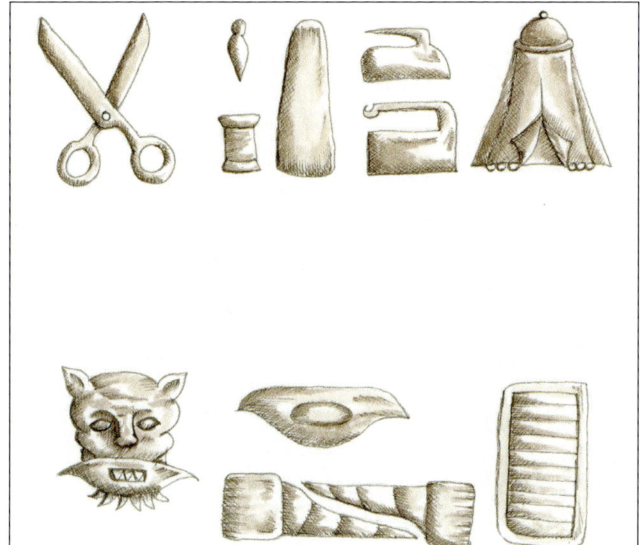

Top: Tailors' symbols, including the goose and flat irons and the trade tent. Bottom: Weavers' trade leopard with shuttle, stretchers and card comb.

Wright

Wright was the eighteenth-century word for an occupation described as a joiner today. The square and compass were common features on their graves, but these would be accompanied by other tools of the trade such as hammers, saws, axes or nails. If the wright had a very specific type of work then this would also be included; for example, if the person was a shipwright then a ship would be included. A fine example of this can be seen at Tulliallen where the wright is carved working on a ship.

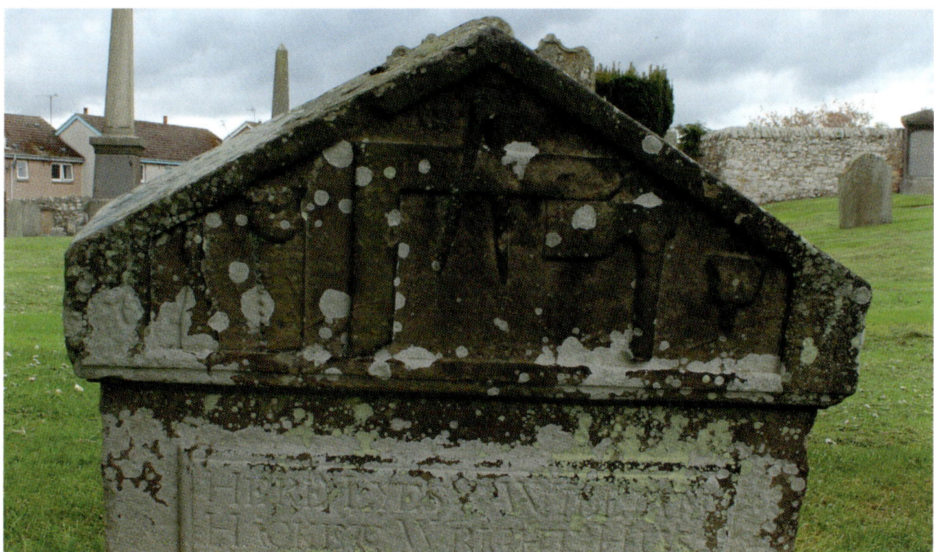

Wright, Ceres.

4

The District of Dunfermline

The presbytery of Dunfermline was established in 1581 at a time when the land was not only economically vibrant but also contained a healthy population. It was a seafaring area with its associated trades of agriculture, cloth manufacture, coal mining and salt works being popular sources of employment for its inhabitants. It is the district of Fife that undertook the fiercest of witch-hunts, and as such it is no surprise to discover the only known grave of a 'witch' to be found in the whole of Scotland is here. The divide between the rich and the poor was startling. Even among the poor there were further divides: coal miners and their families were at one time shunned by other members of the community, being denied burial in some of the parish kirkyards.

Tulliallan

Tulliallan Old Kirkyard, Woodlea, FK10 4PU
The first kirkyard to feature in this book is without doubt one of – if not the – greatest collections of trade symbol gravestones in Scotland. The hard work and dedication of William Wolsey and William Anderson, along with members of the local heritage group, who worked tirelessly to document and reinstall the stones that time had dislodged, is a marvel and an exemplary example for any group interested in reviving and maintaining a historical burial location. As a nation we owe a debt of gratitude to them as so much history has been preserved, and it is a stark reminder of how much has been lost in other such kirkyards.

This is a great place to spend time in any season of the year. To gain access to the kirkyard you must first collect the keys from 'Marco's Kitchen' at the foot of Kirk Street, which is handy as it means you can purchase supplies to warm up or cool down depending on the weather. It is quite the suntrap in the summer, while the damper months really bring out the features of the carvings.

Central to the kirkyard is the roofless kirk, which was built in 1675 and is now a private burial enclosure to the Mitchell family, the last owners of the Tulliallan estate. It was recorded that up to 1933 a mort house once stood in the grounds, though there is no trace of it now. However, the truly mesmerising feature of this burial ground is the row upon row of exquisite gravestones with the trades clearly depicted on their surface. The trades carved or declared in the epitaph cover

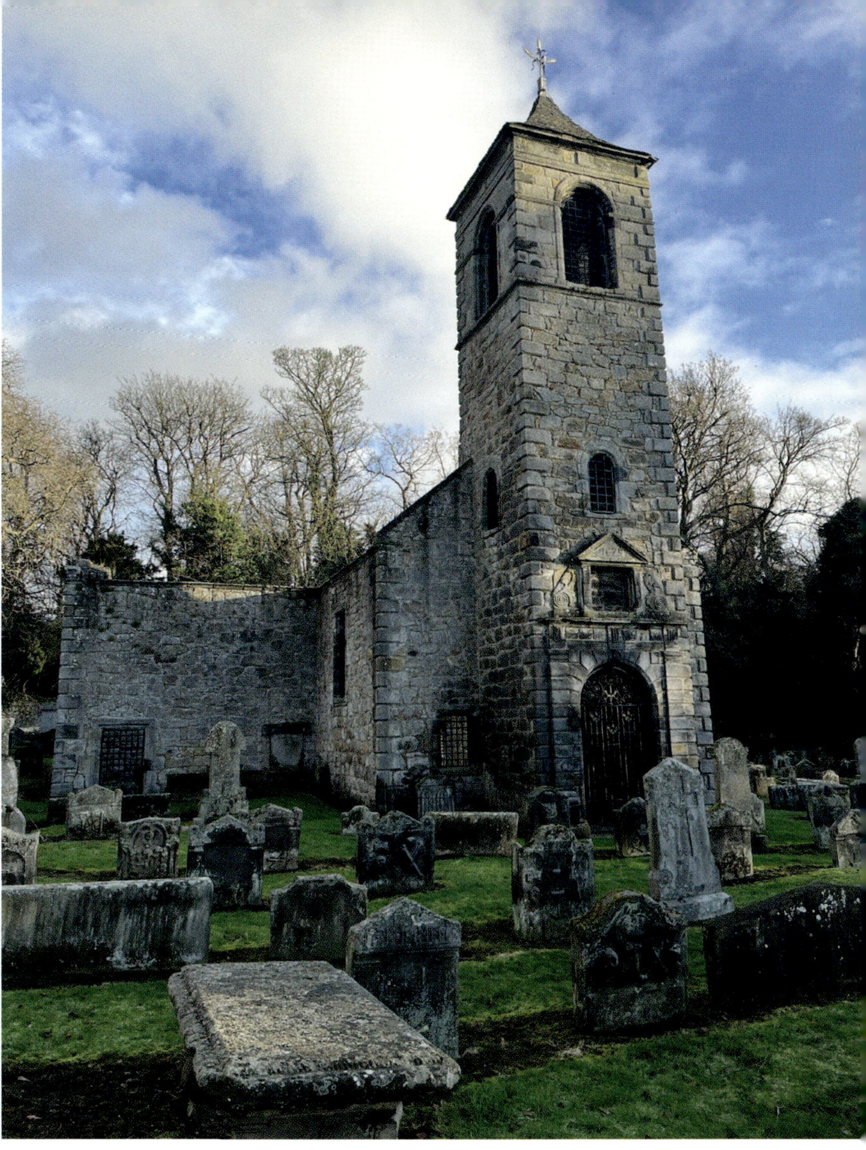

Tulliallan Old Kirk.

fifty-two separate job titles, with the most numerous being shipmasters and other mariner trades. Surprisingly, there is only a single baker.

What is fascinating is the number of gravestones that declare dual trade. One particular stone, belonging to 'J.D.', shows the anchor of a mariner along with a weaver's shuttle, carding comb and stretchers. Shipbuilding and trade were busy at Kincardine, only being surpassed by Leith on the Forth in the eighteenth and nineteenth centuries. However, most of the trade was with the Baltics, an area with the largest expanse of brackish water in the world – due to the amount of freshwater run off from the land it was susceptible to its ports being frozen over. Freezing in the northern extremities would begin in November, with the thaws starting in late April. This meant that for five months of the year a second occupation was required. So when you died why take pride in just one of your trades?!

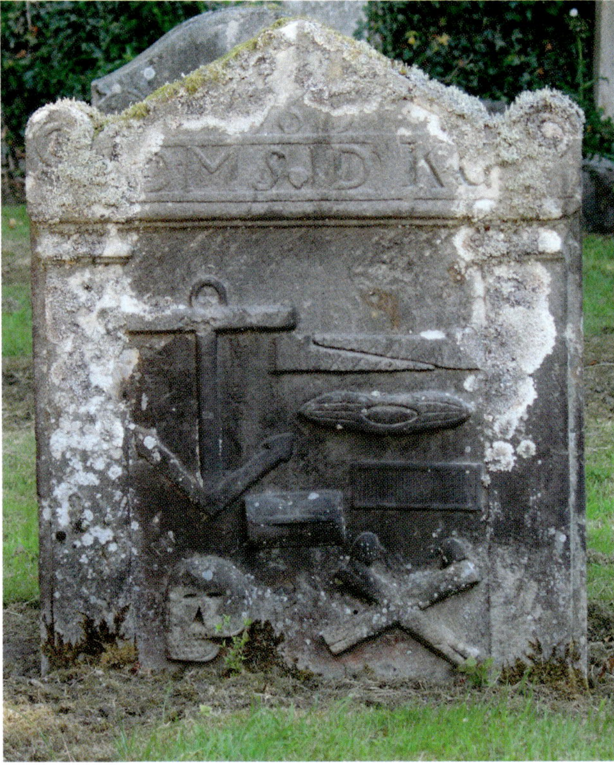

Dual trade stone of a
mariner and weaver.

Culross

Culross Parish Church, Kirk Street, KY12 8JD
Visiting the beautiful little village of Culross is like stepping back in time. It is
easy to see why the location managers of *Outlander* could not resist filming here,
showcasing one of Scotland's most picturesque collections of dwellings to the
world. Its steep, cobbled streets are lined with pantile-rooved houses dating from
the seventeenth century, the names of which give clues as to how their yesteryear
occupants earned their livings; names such as Weavers Cottage, Snuff Cottage
and Old Shoemakers House. Many of the said occupants are eternally resting
in one of the two graveyards of the village, and it is not only the houses that
proudly display their trades but also their graves. The first burial ground can be
found to the rear of Culross Abbey and houses a collection that bears a striking
similarity to Tulliallan. A visit inside the converted 1663 church will reveal the
most magnificent memorial in marble to be found anywhere in Fife: the tomb
of Sir George Bruce of Carnock, who died in 1625. Featured beside him is his
wife Margaret Primrose and eight kneeling statues representing their three sons
and five daughters. Bruce, a merchant and mining engineer, had Culross Palace
built using materials from foreign trade. His innovations in mining brought much
prosperity and trade to the area.

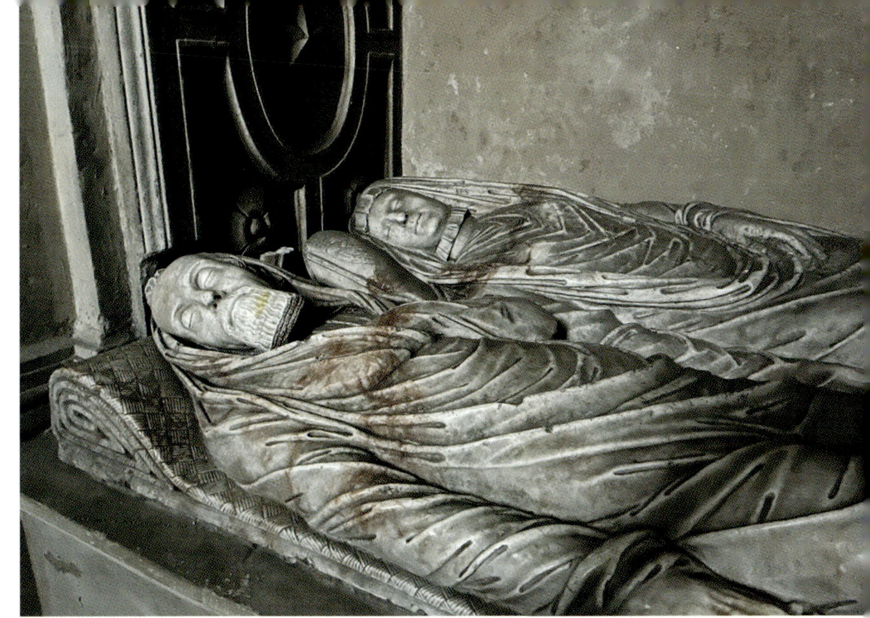

Bruce monument.

The older of the burial grounds is the West Kirk, less than a mile away and used as the Black Kirk in *Outlander*. The kirk was already in a ruinous state in 1675 when four women were accused of being witches before the High Court. What makes this case particularly interesting is that it is almost a perfect textbook witch trial. In fact, it is perhaps a bit too perfect in content and the order of events. All four women – Katherin Sands, Isobelle Inglis, and Agnes and Jonet Hendries – gave near identical confessions of a sabbat at the West Kirk. All of them stated that not only did they

West Kirk, Culross.

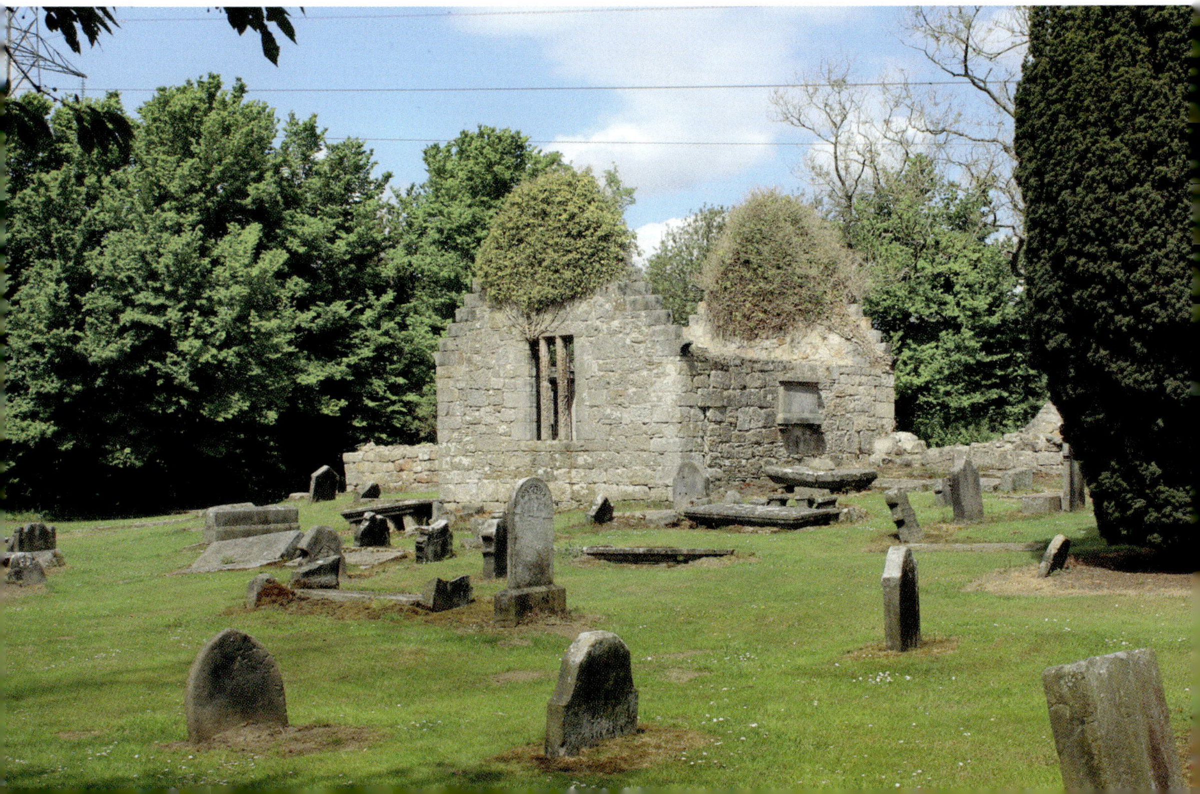

give themselves over to the Devil from head to toe, they then received the Devil's mark and engaged in 'carnal copulation'. Katherin Sands gave a further account that the dead were at one of their meetings and the Devil danced and played a pipe. All the confessions were made in court prior to their executions at the gallows near Leith on 29 July 1675. The rest of the confessions seem to hold elements of a sabbat or the conception of a fairy gathering. In short, it would seem from a modern perspective that the women were manipulated or coached in what to say.

Following the Old Moor Road, west of the West Kirk, a well-used right-of-way path, it leads into the Waas Plantation, which was once moorland as the name suggests. It is along this way that the Plague Grave for the Bald family children is located. It is a beautiful spot shaded in a conifer forest, the air filled with the scent of the pines and, if you keep your eyes focussed and your voices low, you may see one of the red squirrels that inhabit this part of Fife.

One of the most devastating outbreaks of the plague in Scotland was in 1645, a year following catastrophic harvest failures and amid much civil unrest as the Wars of the Three Kingdoms raged on. Suspicion of the cause of the plague fell upon Scottish soldiers arriving back from Newcastle in November 1644. By late spring of 1645 Edinburgh was the epicentre and local government was falling into disarray as nearly half the population was succumbing to the disease. From here it spread out, up the Forth Valley and across to Fife. Culross was particularly affected, though no clear documentation exists. The kirk sessions' last entry

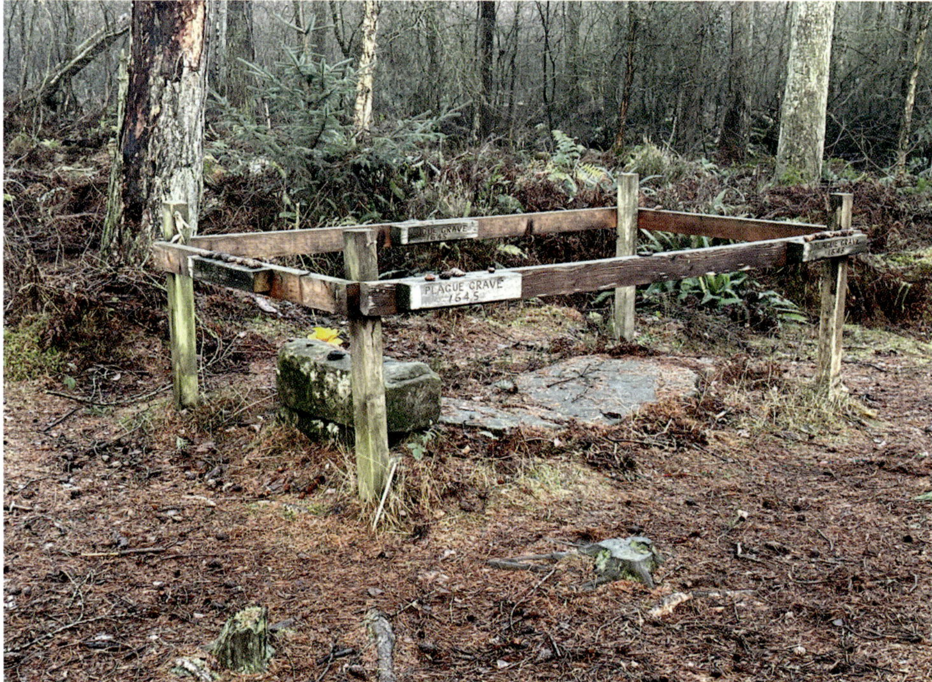

The plague grave of the Bald family children.

was 10 August, when a local man by the name of George was ordered to make public repentance for drunkenness. The next entry was not until January 1646, with the statement: 'During this intermission the plaige was upone our toune.' On 24 September a griddle smith by the name of James Bald lost his three children on the same day – Robert, Agnes and Jean. While it was commonplace to bury plague victims away from the usual parish burial grounds, it was uncommon for a gravestone to mark their final resting place; however, James did just that. The inscription is long gone and the carving of the hammermen trade only just visible. It still attracts caring visitors who from time to time leave flowers, coins, toys or even a pine cone foraged from the floor and placed on the grave or around it.

Torryburn

Torryburn Parish Church, Main Street, KY12 8LT
Torryburn's little parish churchyard in the most tranquil of spots. The smattering of old rowan trees with their bright red berries, symbolising courage and protection, stand guard over their sleeping charges. The stones are mostly covered in moss and lichen with long-since faded inscriptions, leaving the carvings of the trades and imagery of mortality to tell the tales of the lair's owners. There is one stone that portrays a scene from the life of the man who is settled below, and possibly even his wife. It is a tailor's stone from a time where the male-dominated trade shunned women, except where menial and time-consuming tasks were required such as stitching the buttonholes. However, this stone erected for Agnes Hamilton, who died on 10 April 1690, by her tailor husband Andrew Mitchell appears to show the couple working together in unity. Agnes is shown with a full face and the ghost of a smile next to her husband, who looks quite forlorn – they have already been parted after twenty-three years of marriage and two children together.

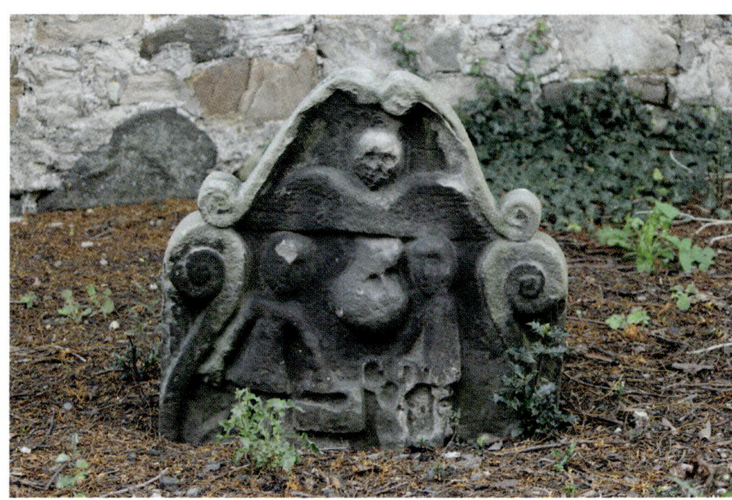

Torryburn
Tailor's grave.

In stark contrast to the idyllic little churchyard burials is down on the mudflats of Torryburn Bay. To the western part of the beach, almost directly in front of the railway bridge, is a large rectangular slab situated halfway between the original high and low tide marks. This indicates the only known grave to a 'witch'. There is an eerie beauty to the location: the oystercatchers calling each other as they fly past over the gentle rippling waters, yet we stand there with the knowledge of the atrocities directed at a poor woman whose only real crime was to perhaps be a little different and old.

Born locally around 1640, Lilias Adie was in her sixties when she was accused of witchcraft on 30 June 1704. She died while imprisoned before she could be formally charged with witchcraft and sentenced to be strangled then burnt at the stake. The authorities, unsure what to do with her body as she had not actually been legally declared a witch, found the solution of burying her in the muddy, waterlogged intertidal section of the beach and placed a large slab over her burial place so she would be unable to rise from her grave. Regrettably, even then she was not allowed to rest peacefully. A century or so later her remains were unearthed, her skull removed to be displayed as a curiosity and parts of her coffin made into walking sticks – one was reputedly given to Andrew Carnegie. Her skull was lost some years ago, but in recent years campaigns have been set up to discover the whereabouts of her remains and to have them returned for a dignified burial.

Lilias Adie's grave in Torryburn Bay.

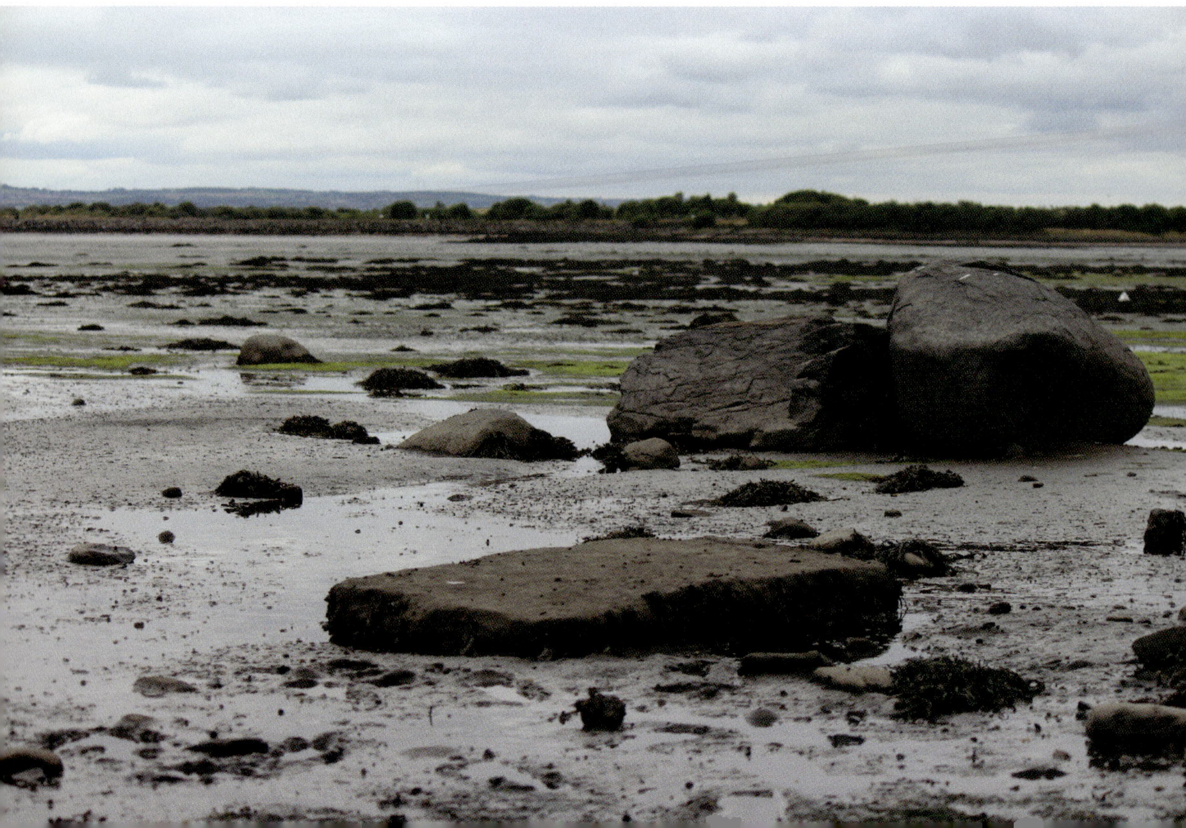

Limekilns

Rosyth Old Kirk, Near Brucehaven Road, Limekilns, KY11 3JR
Contrary to the name and location of Rosyth today, you go into Limekilns and down Brucehaven Road to reach the path east of the village. This leads to the graveyard surrounding Rosyth Old Parish Kirk – a ruin by 1775. During the nineteenth century Thomas Bruce, Earl of Elgin and Kincardine, granted the parish extra land for burial, extending the graveyard to the north and west. The mort house is to the right upon entrance. The congregation of Rosyth were particularly fearful due to the excessive activities of the Edinburgh Resurrectionists, with tales of boats rowing across the Forth to steal the dead. In 1825, a meeting was called to discuss a solution. It resulted in the agreement that a mort house was necessary and would be paid for by subscription. Those who paid a subscription had priority use. The laws and regulations of the mort house were:

1. The coffin used must be made of foreign wood, three-fourths of an inch thick, the inside run or coated with pitch, a round of cloth fixed on the top and joining of the lid and the lid properly screwed down. 2. The time allowed to remain in the vault to be two months in summer and three months in winter. 3. The poor may have the benefit of the vault, gratis, by giving a preference to subscribers on all occasions. 4. Non-subscribers using the vault shall pay half a Guinea for an adult above 18 years and five shillings below that age.

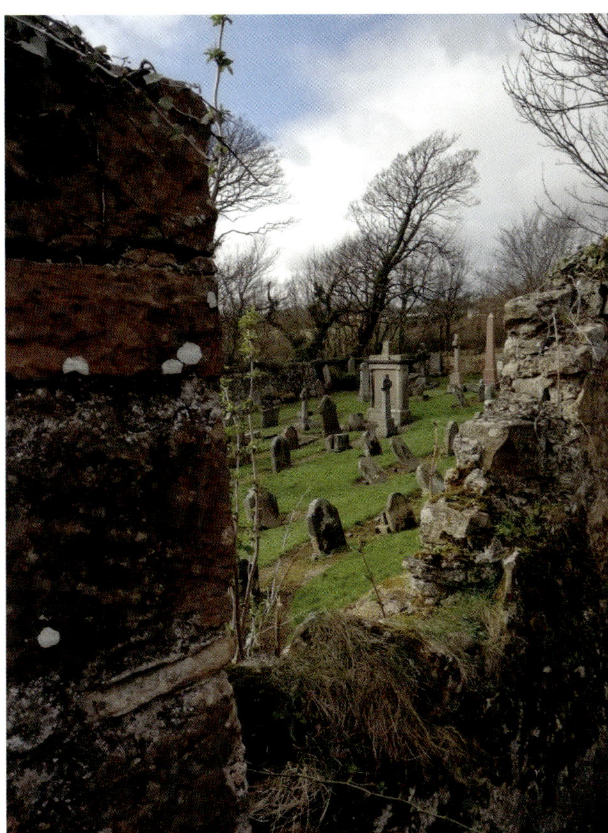

Rosyth Old Kirkyard.

As you stroll around the grounds here inspecting the graves, which date from the seventeenth century, you may notice objects rather more modern. These are little salt-glazed brick markers next to the memorial stones. Rather than being random bricks etched with the number and glazed, these were tapered at one end for ease of insertion into the soil then individually stamped and fired. Unfortunately, there is no manufacturer's mark on the bricks, so it is difficult to date them; although, due to the popularity of their use it is most likely to have been early in the last century. Salt-glazed bricks can withstand weather conditions considerably better than their unglazed counterparts and, as such, these are still looking super and look to last at least another century or so.

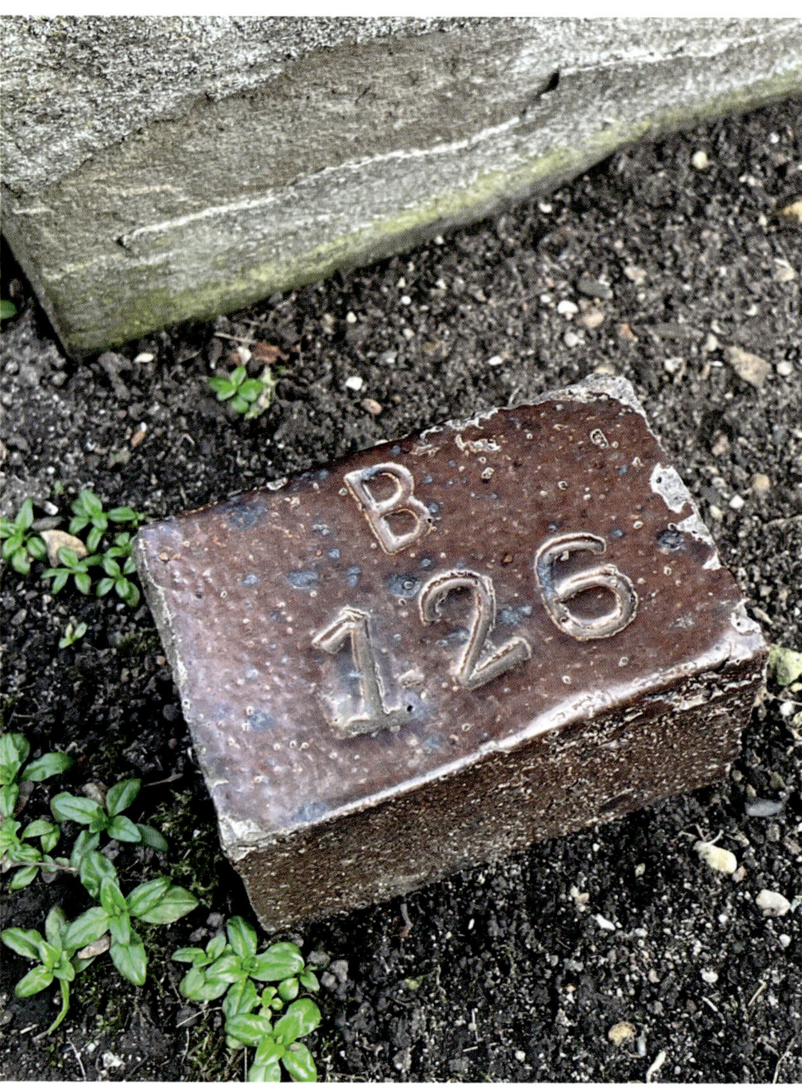

Salt-glazed brick grave marker.

North Queensferry

St James Parish Churchyard, Chapel Place, North Queensferry, KY11 1HE
The most curious of small graveyards can be found in North Queensferry. It was
the site of the first place of worship pilgrims would come to after crossing the Forth
at the Queens Ferry. The storms and currents made the passage across the water
a perilous task, so David I granted the Abbot of Dunfermline 'passage and ship of
Endekeithin' in 1129. The ferrying of passengers eventually became too much for
the monks and the role was taken on by substantial seamen, who were used to the
conditions of the Forth. It would seem, however, that the sailors were starting to
charge ever-increasing and conflicting amounts, which led to Parliament fixing a
flat fee of 1*d* per person and 2*d* per horse in 1474.

There was a change in management again in 1589 when James VI gave the fourteen-
year-old Anne of Denmark the governance of the ferry as a wedding gift. Meanwhile,
the little Church of St James continued to be used for worship until the building
became ruinous in the late sixteenth century. Rather than build a new church those
who dwelled in the parish would either travel to Inverkiething or cross the Forth.
The sailors of North Queensferry had a loft at St Peter's Church in Inverkeithing
where they would worship together and eventually they would gain their own burial
ground to be buried together. In 1752, the Sailors' Society were granted the remains
of the chapel and little burial yard for their own. They built a wall around it and
identified it with their own marker: 'This is done by the sailers in north ferrie 1752'.

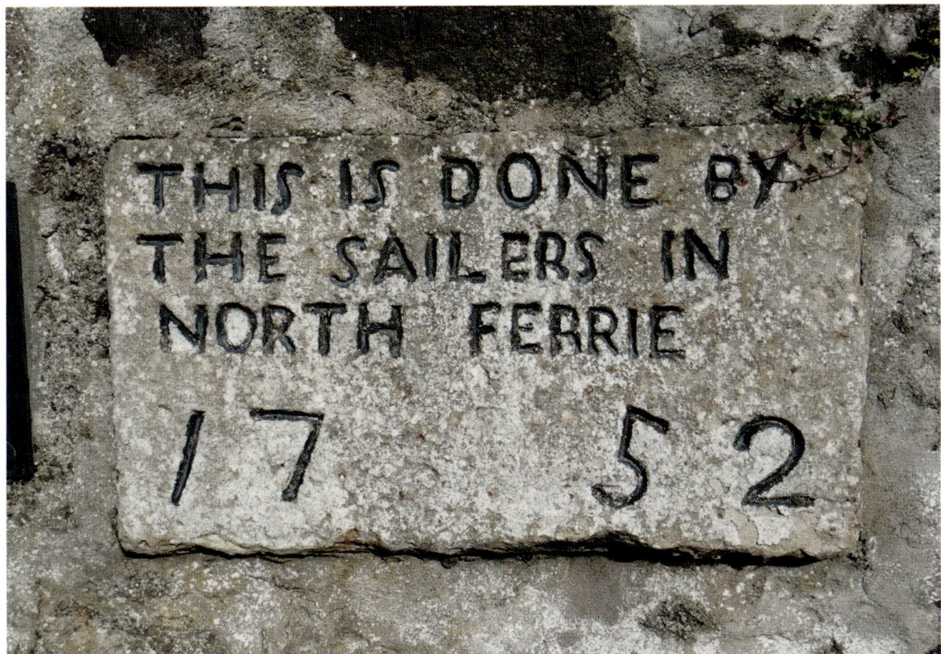

South Queensferry sailors' graveyard.

Dalgety Bay

To many unaware of the history of the area, Dalgety Bay is considered to be a 'new town' due to the mass construction of housing taking place from 1965. However, taking a walk along the costal path and to the east of the town you will come across the beautiful medieval ruin of St Bridget's Kirk, the church once at the heart of the long-gone village of Dalgetty. The oldest parts of this building date from 1178 when it was recorded that Pope Alexander III issued a papal bull that called for the founding of the 'Church at Dalgetty with its appurtenances'. It was reconsecrated and dedicated to St Bridget in 1244, with the religious services arranged by the canons of Inchcolm Abbey right up until the Reformation of 1560. The building was expanded and altered after this date to adhere to Protestant worship. In the early seventeenth century four aisles were added by prominent local families. The aisle to the south is mostly rubble and its family connection has been lost over time. To the north are two aisles for the families of Fordell and Inglis of Otterston. To the left of the gated Inglis Aisle can be seen mounted in the wall the beautiful marker to Elizabeth Heriot, wife of William Ingles of Otteston, who died in 1621. The crest bears the clam shells of the Heriot's crest and the demi-lion of the Inglis.

The grandest of the aisles is to the west of the building: the Dunfermline Aisle, built on the instructions of Alexander Seton, 1st Earl of Dunfermline, presumably after the death of his first wife, Lilias Drummond, on 8 May 1601. He was the first to be buried in what is now the family burial vault under the Lairds Loft, which can be accessed by an external doorway to the north of the building. Winding up the stairs, you are greeted by a well-sized room and a retiring room complete with a fireplace to the rear and splendid views out over the Forth.

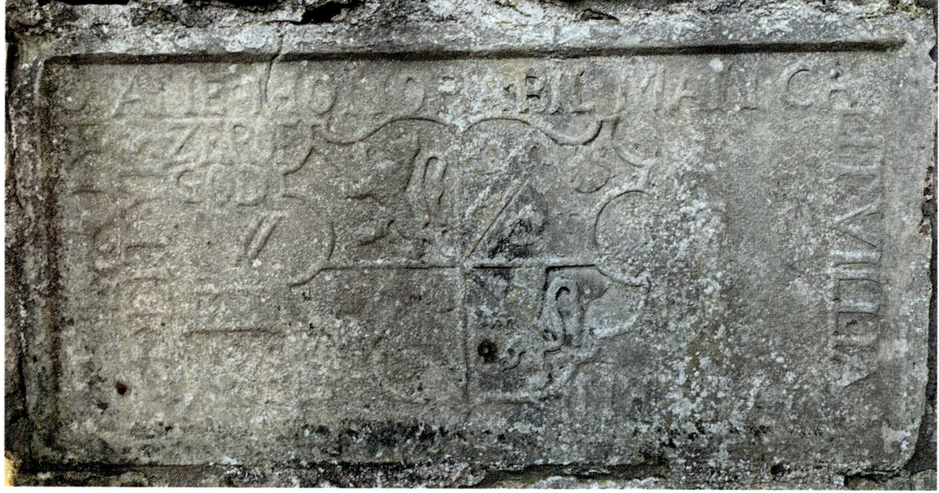

Elizabeth Heriot, 1621.

Not only is Lilias one of the earl's wives who was laid to rest here (if rest is what it can be called), but she is perhaps the most famous of them due to tales of her ghost – the Green Lady of Fyvie – haunting Fyvie Castle in Aberdeenshire, wandering the halls and accompanied by the smell of roses. Legend goes that, many years before, a curse was put upon Fyvie Castle that no male heirs of any current laird would be born there. Seton and Lilias had five daughters born at the castle before she mysteriously fell ill and died at her husband's home in Dalgetty without any male issue and was buried at the nearby church. Just five months later Seton married his next, younger wife – Grizel Leslie of Rothes. On their wedding night at the infamous castle they were disturbed by mournful moans and scratching noises, though no source could be found. The next morning the name 'D. Lilias Drumond' was found carved into the stonework of the external window ledge, which is 50 feet from the ground and can still be seen today. By 1607, Grizel was dead and had been interred at Dalgetty. Seton then married his third wife, Margaret Hay, who not only bore him a son, Charles Seton (2nd Earl of Dunfermline) and two more daughters, but managed to outlive her husband, who died on 16 June 1622.

St Bridget's Kirk.

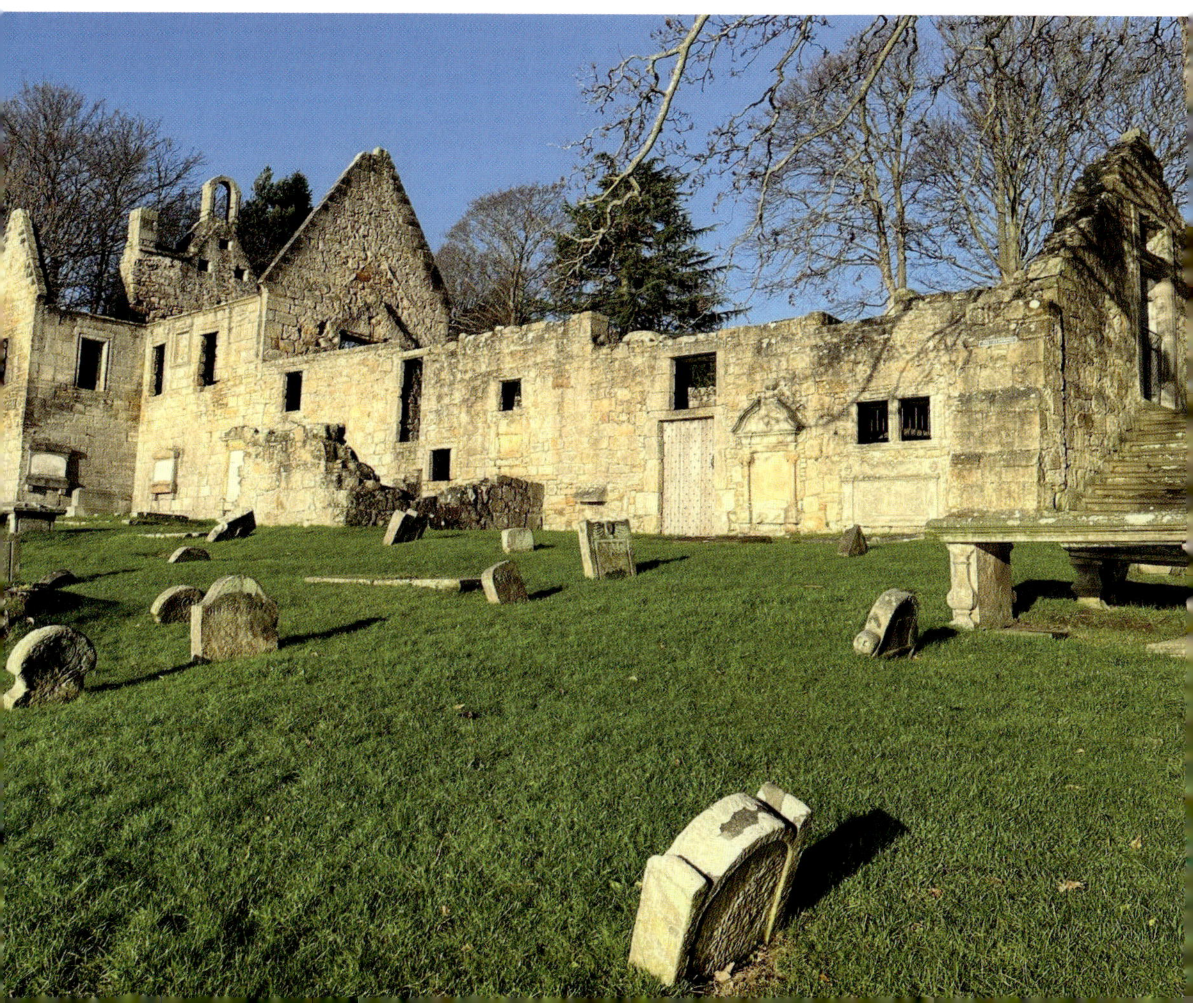

Outside in the kirkyard there are a number of interesting seventeenth- and eighteenth-century stones. Though weathered by their location so close to the sea, they still hold much charm and character and deserve more than a passing glance. One memorial in particular stands out for its unique charm. The Bathgate family table stone can be found at the eastern edge of the grounds. It's hard not to read between the lines when looking at this grave with its unique, quirky additions and assume that it was a parents love that wanted death to be less scary for their children, as on closer inspection two rather comical yet kind little faces gaze back at you. Revd Mr James Bathgate, Minister of the Gospel at Dalgety, married Euphane Anderson of the parish of Aberdour on 12 November 1741. Their first child, Agnes, was born in 1743, followed by Margaret (1744), Janet (1745), Helen (1746) and James (1748). Sadly, between 1744 and 1750 their daughters had all died and were buried in the kirkyard. Where many other gravestones nearby are decorated with the expected symbols of mortality, these warm, friendly faces decorate two of the scrolls, which stand roughly at a height a small child would be able to see. Euphane joined her daughters on 8 July 1755. Revd James Bathgate never remarried and when he died on 23 December 1776 he was still the minister at Dalgety, having never moved away from his family.

Towards the central coast area of Dalgety Bay is another curious building that seems out of place, nestled in a patch of green and trees among large modern houses. This is the mortuary chapel of the earls of Moray, who were once owners of the Donibristle estate, which the town of Dalgety Bay is now established upon. Roofless and gated, it is the final resting place for eleven of the Stuart family in

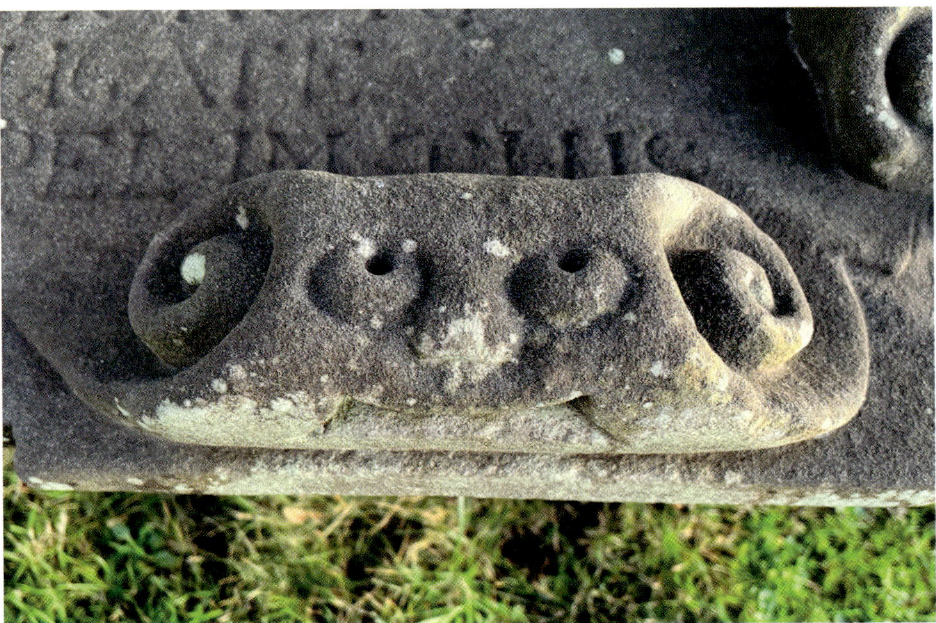

Face detail on the Bathgate table monument.

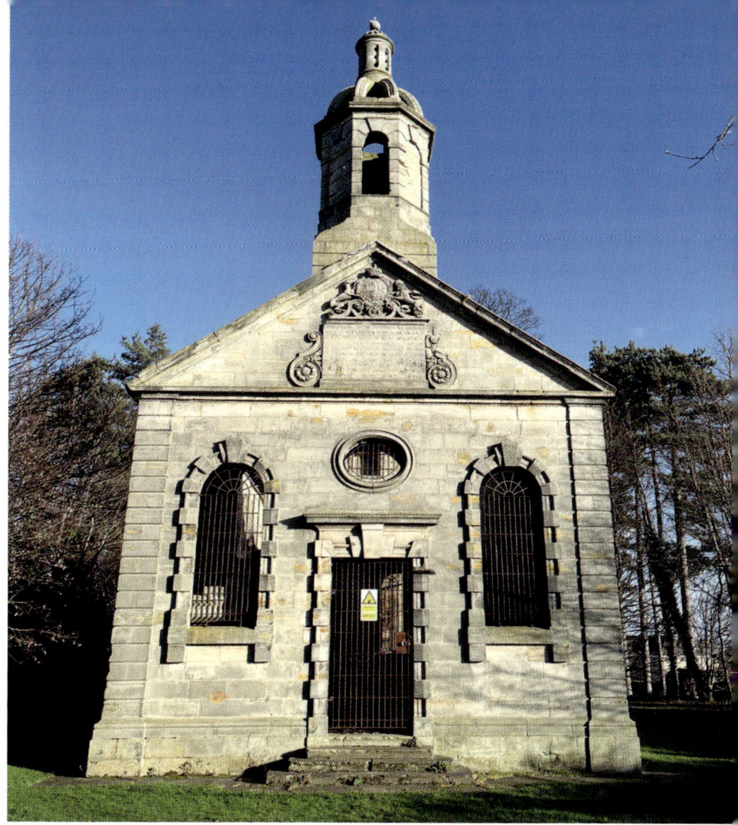

Moray Chapel.

the vault below, nine of whom are earls – from Charles Stuart, 6th Earl of Moray, interred there in 1735, down through successive earls until George Philip Stuart, 14th Earl of Moray, 160 years later in 1895.

Dunfermline

Dunfermline Abbey Graveyard, St Margaret Street, Dunfermline, KY12 7PE
Walking around the well-kept grounds of the abbey graveyard often leads to people gazing up at the buildings. At its centre are the nineteenth-century church with the words 'King Robert the Bruce' at its crown and the twelfth-century nave; in fact, the graves are almost an afterthought once the further buildings of the ruined refectory, Dunfermline Palace and the eye-catching pink of the rear of Abbot House are also taken in.

This is the very heart of Dunfermline's heritage. With seven confirmed kings (though some say eight or even nine), some of their queen consorts (one of whom was canonised as St Margaret of Scotland) and several princes, it is one of the most populated royal burial places on mainland Scotland – surpassed only by Iona. Within the church, under the pulpit, is a brass marker showing where Robert the Bruce is interred. This clearly explains why his name is built into the design on the building, with it almost acting like a fitting memorial chapel to perhaps Scotland's most famous king.

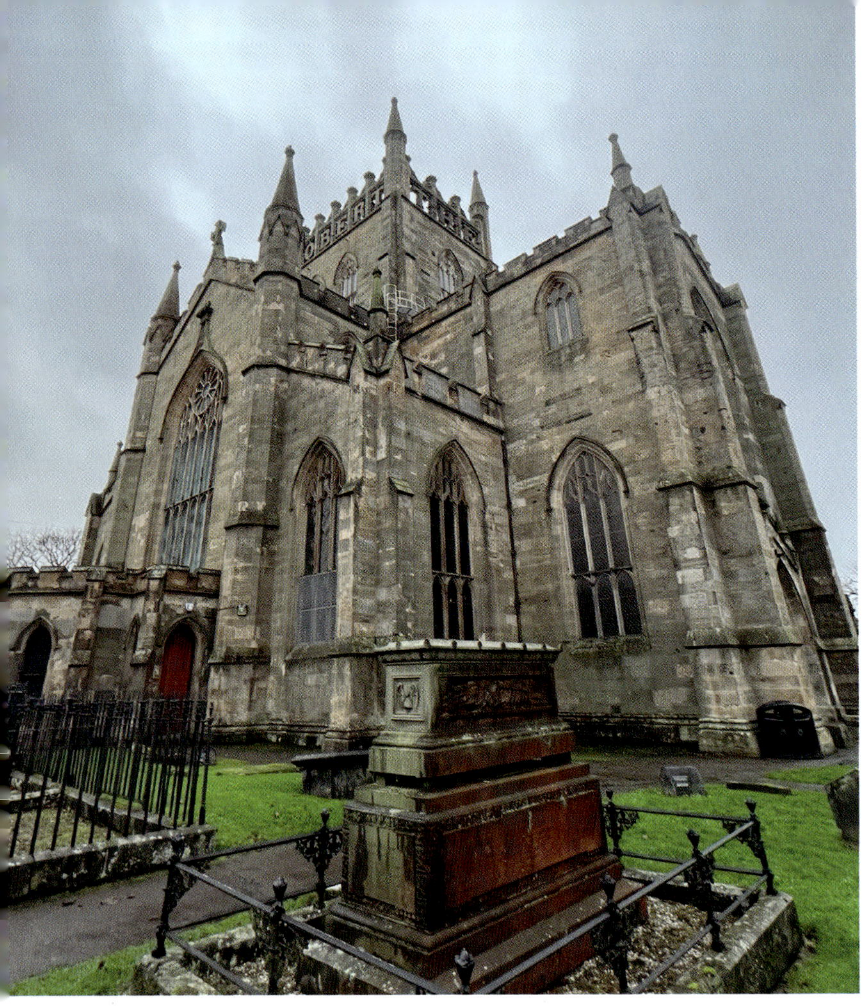

Dunfermline Abbey
Church.

While it may be argued that Mary, Queen of Scots is Scotland's most famous queen, there is another contender; however, it is really her status as a saint as opposed to a queen that she is famed for. This is the saintly queen Margaret, an English princess born in Hungary and the second wife of Malcolm III. She is credited as bringing the Roman Catholic faith into Scotland and displacing the Culdee Church when she successfully invited a community of Benedictine monks from Canterbury to establish a monastery in Dunfermline. Her son, David I, would go on to make the priory an abbey in 1128. Also referred to as 'the Pearl of Scotland', she was well known for her piety and charity, traits she would influence her husband and children with. Perhaps her most lasting achievement was the establishment of the Queen's Ferry across the Forth, providing safe crossing for pilgrims on their way to St Andrews. There is also the Queensferry Crossing today, which can be driven over, and when names were being considered for the new bridge St Margaret's Crossing was shortlisted as one of the possible names.

Dying in Edinburgh on 16 November 1093, just three days after her husband and eldest son were killed at the Battle of Alnwick, Margaret's body was taken across the Forth to Dunfermline and buried before the high altar. In 1250, Pope

Innocent IV canonised her and her remains were reinterred in a magnificent, highly decorated wooden casket upon fossil-rich Frosterly marble from County Durham – a special type of limestone that can be polished to a high shine. This part is all that remains of the shrine.

Along with the miracles associated with St Margaret's, fertility and protection during childbirth were deemed the most important to many women. Having borne eight children herself, future queens would also call upon her for help. Margaret Tudor sent for 'Sanet Margaretis Sark' (her shirt), while her granddaughter, Mary, Queen of Scots, sent for the bejewelled casket containing Margaret's head for the birth of her son, James VI. During the Reformation the head inside its casket were said to have been taken to France for protection, but there have been no confirmed sightings of it since the French Revolution.

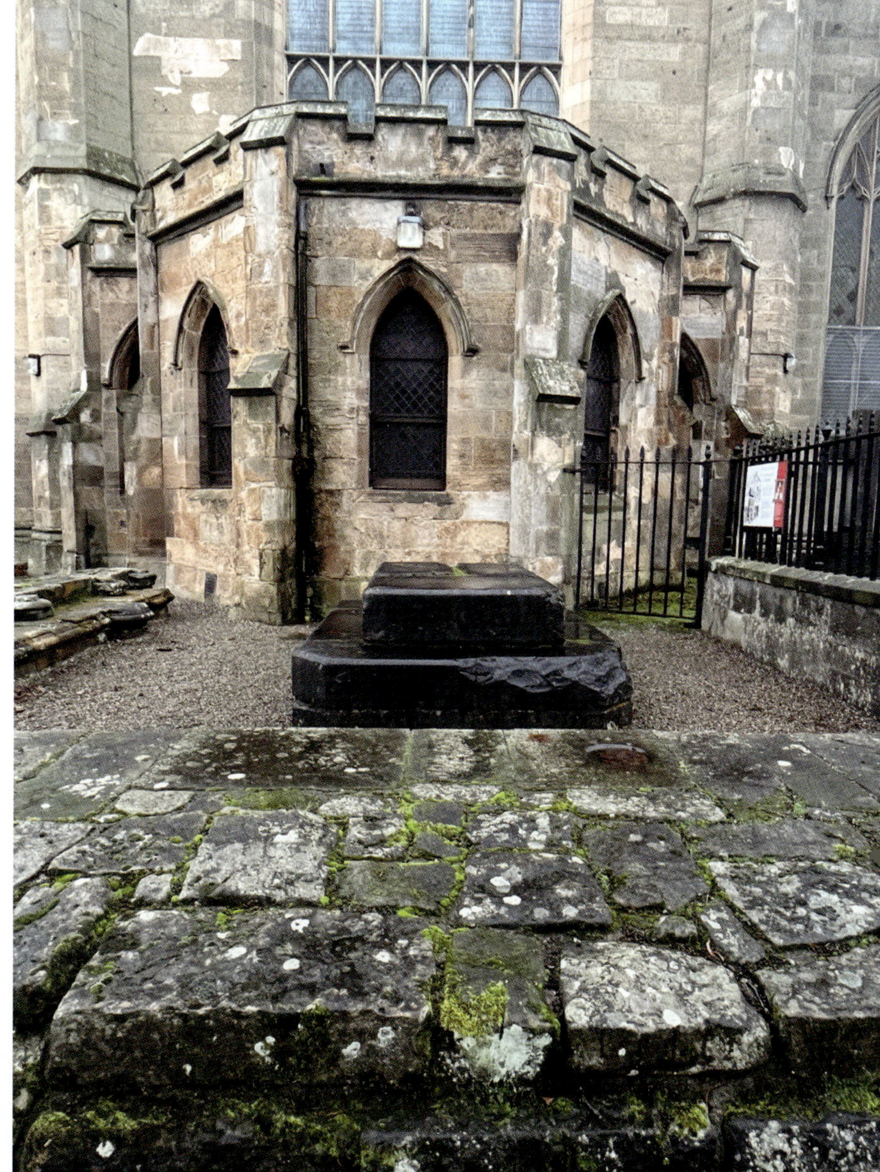

St Margaret's
shrine.

Dunfermline Abbey's graveyard comprises two sections. The northern area was used for around 800 years until its final burial in 1896. The area south of the abbey church was used after the completion of the new building in 1823 and, while still in use into the mid-twentieth century, there was a decline in interments after the opening of the Halbeath Cemetery in 1863, as people opted for the ever-popular location of the new garden cemeteries. During the Victorian period there was an increasing trend across Scotland for cemeterial burial rather than the traditional (and often vastly overcrowded) parish burial grounds. Urban sanitation and public health were of growing concern during this period, and people were encouraged to use cemeteries with incentives such as cheaper plots and a reduction in fees for funerals that used a hearse rather than the traditional walking funeral. Inevitably, this change of location, often outside the town or city limits, meant the funerals themselves changed along with the attendants.

A look back through newspaper articles brings up some interesting pieces about funerals and changing attitudes in Dunfermline, with one in particular published in the *Fifeshire Journal* on 18 September 1844. The grounds of the graveyard are particularly praised, with credit being given to Mr Allan, the superintendent who had created a delightful landscape with new shrubs and flowerpots. However, the author goes on to berate a funeral procession, condemning 'practices which could only be tolerated through habit'. The number of attendees is complimented, there being over fifty people all attired most respectfully in their clothing – so far, so good. It is the manner in which the mourners conduct themselves that brings the stinging rebuke, as they walk to the graveyard in a 'most disorderly manner … the greatest unconcern is evident and every manner of conversation is carried on – politics, weather, trade, the price of cattle, are all discussed'. If this was not enough, the horror continues for the observer. When the group entered the churchyard many rushed forward to inspect the depth of the grave, blocking the way for the attendants carrying the coffin. While the author was scandalised, it is a wonderful window into the past that acts as a reminder that while Dunfermline is famed for its royal and saintly connections, it is also the last stop for the ordinary folk of the town who have their place in the woven fabric of its history.

A casual glance at the headstones reveals a myriad of untold stories, and it isn't just headstones on view. In January 2022, workmen digging up the path by the north door came across stones that have lain beneath the path for decades, raising the question of just how much of our untold local history lies written beneath the soil.

It is not just the buildings and headstones that deserve attention as these burial grounds also play host to one of Scotland's ultimate figures of legend and folk stories – or at least his mother. Many people pass by the unassuming hawthorn tree; however, by inspecting the little plaque it reveals that this is the spot where Sir William Wallace's mother, Lady Margaret Crawford, is buried. There are no records that give credence to this claim, but various writers through the centuries since have kept up the narrative. Blind Harry describes Margaret and Wallace

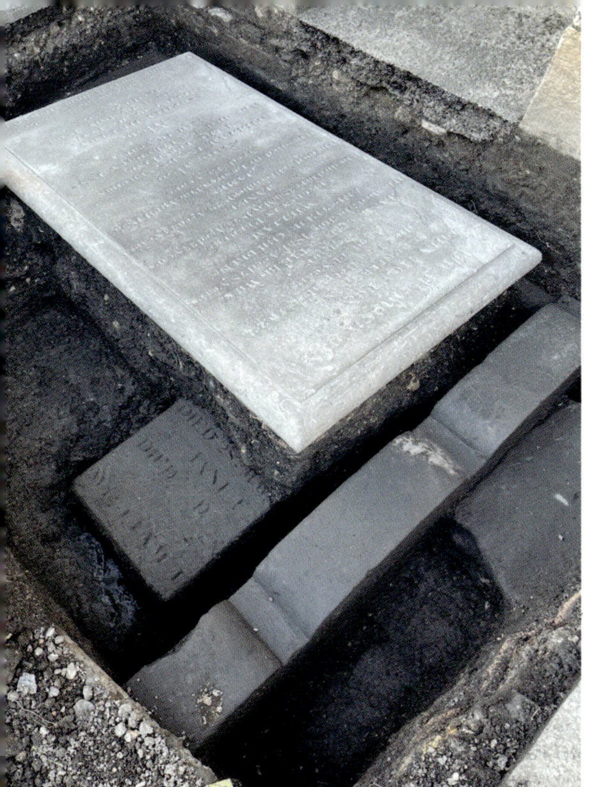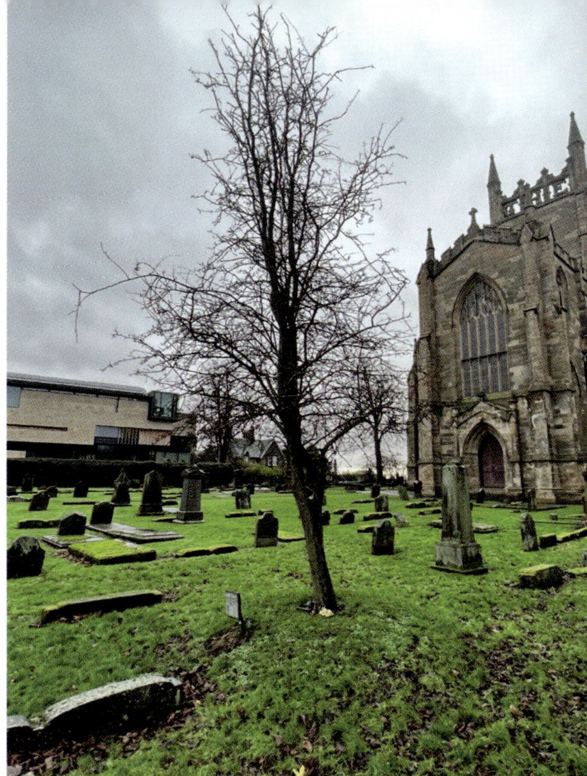

Above left: Rediscovered graves in Dunfermline.

Above right: Reputed site of William Wallace's mother's grave.

disguising themselves as pilgrims when it was deemed perilous to remain in Ayrshire after a young Wallace killed Governor Selby's son in an argument in 1296: 'His mother clad herself in Pilgrims weed, then him disguis'd and both marched off with speed.' While it is unlikely that was when Margaret died, it is known that Wallace was in Dunfermline in 1297. In the annals of Dunfermline of that year it is recorded that a monk of the Benedictine cloister of Dunfermline, Arnold Blair, left to become chaplain to Sir William Wallace.

It is likely that Margaret's death was in 1303. Wallace made the Forest of Dunfermline his hiding place and had already been branded a traitor by Edward I. It is believed that it was at this time Margaret died and, rather than being buried in the church, was buried anonymously to save her remains from the vengeful attentions of Edward. A returning visitor, the English king spent the winter of 1303/04 at Dunfermline Abbey. However, it would seem he was a rather ungracious guest as he set it alight when he left! The original hawthorn tree was said to have blown down at the turn of the nineteenth century and replaced with cuttings. Another storm was to take that tree around a hundred years later and cuttings were used again. This is the tree that is still seen today.

5

The District of Kirkcaldy

The presbytery of Kirkcaldy dates from 1593 and sits nestled within the other three, its geography of both the contrasting hills and the south-central coastline. Mining, maritime, industry and trade all fit together, adapting and modernising up and into the twentieth century. Regrettably, some of the kirkyards within this area have lost many of their old stones through removal, with ancient churches now central to much newer gravestones. It is a misconception that people buy their burial land, rather they purchase a 'Grant of Exclusive Right of Burial' for a grave space with a term of fifty years within council-owned graveyards and cemeteries, with whom ownership remains. While there is a level of disappointment from a heritage point of view, there is a case for reuse of burial spaces, especially for people who wish to be buried in parish churchyards.

Burntisland

Kirkton Old Church, Church Street, KY3 0EX
Little remains of the twelfth-century church dedicated to St Serf in the lands once known as Parva Kinghorn, a fishing hamlet and part of Kinghorn. In the 1500s the little settlement gained its independence and became Burntisland. The kirk is the oldest building in the town, even in its ruinous state. What remains are the nave, chancel and south aisle, which had been the main place of worship and burial until 1592 and the building of the new parish church. It continued to be used for worship by those who lived close by until the mid-1600s, though burial continued until the twentieth century. The very last burial was Helen MacKinnon, who died at the age of ninety on 30 May 1936. The grounds had been closed for interment; however, a special dispensation was made for Helen and the grounds were opened for one final burial so she could be laid to rest beside her late husband, John Donaldson.

While there are fascinating examples of older markers in the grounds and within the kirk, there is a nineteenth-century monument situated on the wall of the ruinous kirk that requires further inspection. It belongs to Gordon MacDonald, one time owner of the Moy Plantation at Coronie in Surinam, who died in Burntisland on 28 June 1859. Interred there is his daughter Classina Mary

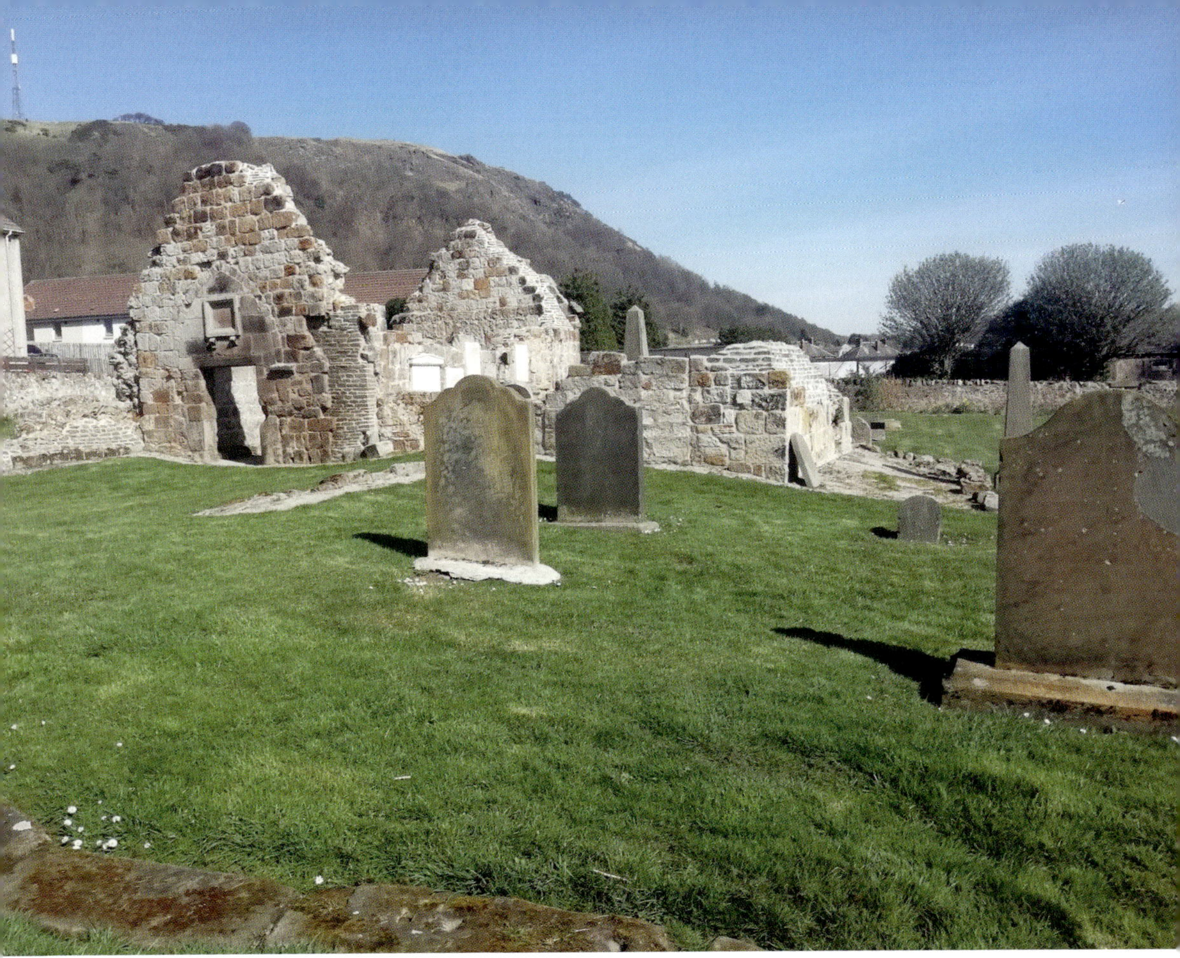

Kirkton Old Churchyard.

MacDonald, who had been born Catherina, an enslaved person, at Hamilton, the neighbouring plantation to her father's. Her mother was a domestic enslaved lady called Mary. MacDonald first arrived in Surinam in 1848, working as a director for a plantation there before buying the plantation of Moy in 1853, which included around 130 enslaved people as part of the purchase. Buying shares in other plantations, he seemed to settle there until April 1858 when he suddenly returned to Burntisland. His daughter Catherina was manumitted that same year and her name later changed to Classina Mary MacDonald, though it is unclear if she travelled to Scotland with her father. MacDonald died fourteen months later and his estates were sold, leaving Classina financially secure for the rest of her life, of which little is known. She didn't need to seek employment and she never married, spending time in Nairn, yet she was in Edinburgh during the 1881 census. She died at Strathtay, in the company of her nurse, of acute peritonitis in 1906 at the age of fifty-one and was buried with her father in Burntisland. In 2018, she was included in the New Biographical Dictionary of Scottish Women.

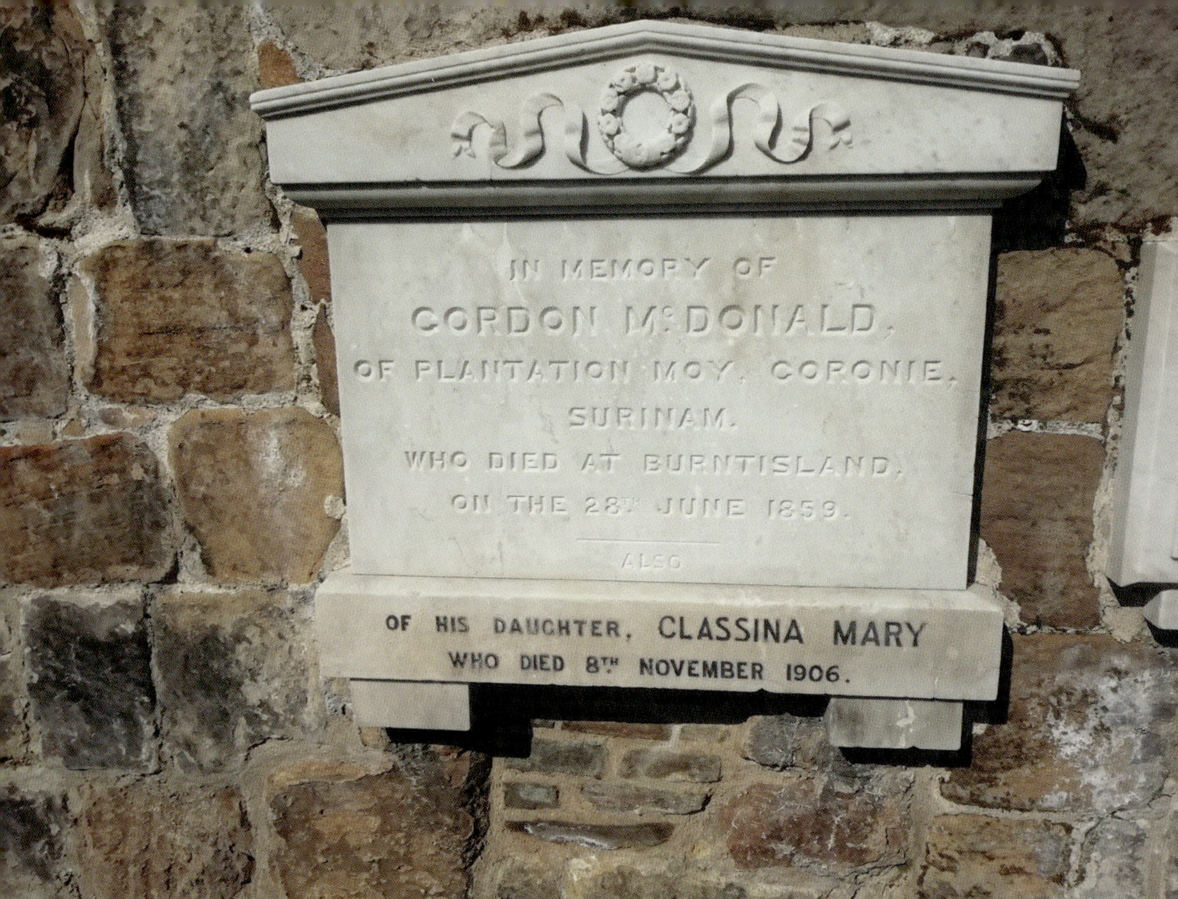

McDonald memorial.

Burtisland Parish Church, Leven Street, KY3 9DH
During the sixteenth century Burtisland had grown considerably, achieving royal burgh status in 1568. The townspeople wanted to symbolise their prosperity in a fitting way so started raising funds to build a new church to replace Kirkton as its main place of worship. Situated on higher ground, it overlooks the town's once bustling harbour. Finally opening for worship in 1592, it is one of Scotland's earliest post-Reformation churches. It was here that a momentous moment in church history took place. On 12 May 1601, the General Assembly of the Church of Scotland met here due to an outbreak of the plague in Edinburgh. It was apparently at this assembly that James VI requested a new version of the Bible be created, leading to the authorised King James Bible.

The gates to the grounds can be opened by prior arrangement with the church, though they are also open on Sundays when there is a church service. The grounds are worth waiting for access as they house a treasure trove of monuments rich in detail and script – in a way many emulate some of the graveyard monuments of Edinburgh. There is one monument that is quite poignant, which is dedicated to a man who was not considered a great man yet was a greatly appreciated one. At the top of the stone is a carving of a barefooted man, a tammie upon his head and wearing a thick coat and trousers turned up at the hem, pushing a wooden wheelbarrow. This is the grave of George Arnot, a dock worker who was considered an exceptionally likeable man, quick to tell a joke or sing a song. During sermons he was able to memorise the whole service and repeat it in entirety to others. Little else is known about him, but his premature death was seemingly been a prank gone wrong: he was poisoned after being given a glass of whiskey laced with snuff. After his death a public competition was run to write a poem that best described him. The poem was then added to his monument, which was paid for by public subscription:

Erected by Subscribers
To the Memory of George Arnot
as a token of respect to him
for his usefulness to the public
He died there 27th March 1850 aged 35 years
His mind was weak, his body strong,
His answer ready with a song,
A mem'ry like him few could boast
Yet suddenly his life he lost.

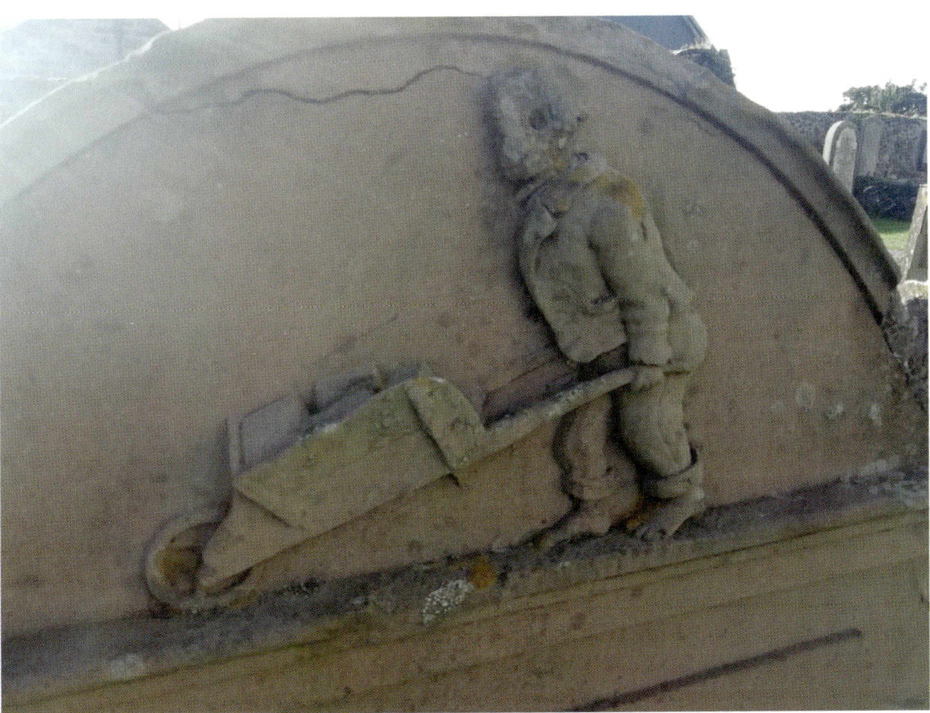

George Arnot at Burntisland Parish Church.

Auchtertool

Auchtertool Kirk, Off B925 Road, KY2 5XH
The kirkyard of Auchtertool is quite isolated and has been described as 'one of the most quiet and retired of places'. Situated on a hill, the views across the fields to the Firth of Forth bring a certain peace to the soul – a chance to step away from modern life. Being so isolated, its position also attracted the attention of resurrectionists in the early eighteenth century. The minister who lived in the manse, the kirk's only neighbour, was often away from home on parish business, leaving opportunist rogues the chance to carry out their macabre harvesting with little to no challenge. The situation came to a head after a local ploughman was returning home across the fields at about midnight. The next day he reported hearing strange noises and seeing lights from the kirkyard. An investigation revealed a fresh grave had been disturbed belonging to the daughter of the minister's housekeeper. A meeting was called and in 1830 the heads of local households formed the Auchtertool Mortsafe Association. Funds were raised for two iron coffins – one large and one small – to be placed over coffins of the newly deceased. Further precautions were taken with the use of janker stones, one of which still sits against the boundary wall of the kirkyard. The minutes from the session record that guards from the association would also patrol the area with firearms as part of the protection of deceased members; non-members, however, were charged from £1 10s for this protection. Although the Anatomy Act of 1832 meant the end of the trade of bodies, the association was not dissolved until 1853.

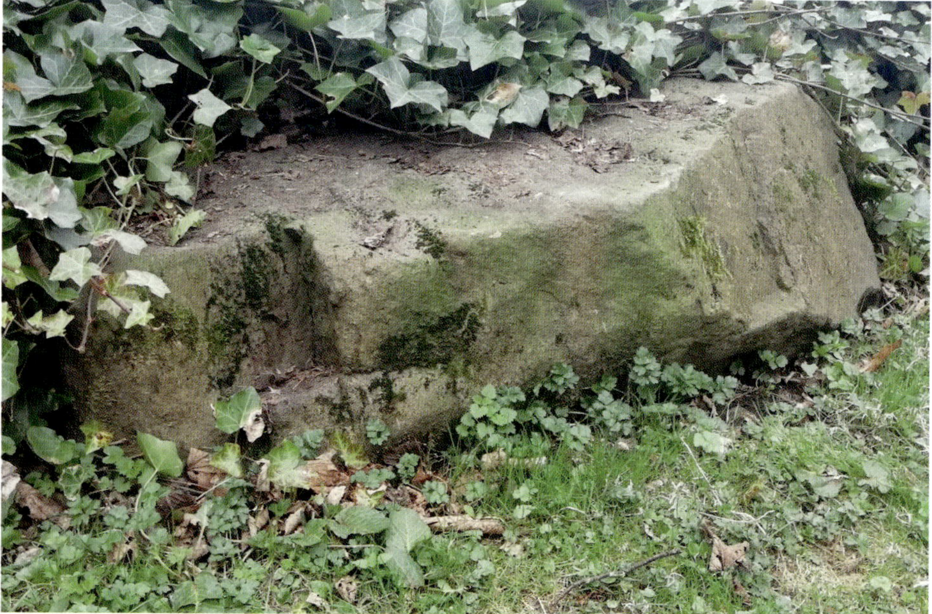

Janker stone at Auchtertool.

Kirkcaldy

Kirkcaldy Old Kirk, Kirk Wynd, KY1 1EH
The first written record for the church building here was its consecration in 1244, though it has been a site for Christian worship since the seventh century when the Celtic Catholic missionaries came from Ireland. The tower is now the oldest part of the church, dating from the fifteenth century. Since 2011 the building has belonged to Kirkcaldy Old Kirk Trust after its sale by the Church of Scotland and provides an important centre for community use, historical research and concerts while also retaining worship for local groups.

The most famous person to be buried here has a memorial and stained-glass window inside the kirk building. Born on 21 January 1613, Revd George Gillespie became a leading church and statesman, eloquent in both preaching and debate. He was the youngest member of the Westminster Assembly of Divines and it was he, as one of the authors, who presented the Westminster Confession of Faith to the General Assembly on 4 August 1647, obtaining its ratification. Having been the minister of Greyfriars Kirk in Edinburgh since 1641, he was elected to the High Kirk of St Giles in September 1647 and further elected Moderator of the Assembly on 12 July 1648. His health became a cause of concern, however, and he returned to Kirkcaldy to recuperate but died on 17 December of tuberculosis at the age of just thirty-five.

He was buried outside the walls of the kirk, in keeping with the Presbyterian practice, and a simple headstone was installed. However, due to his fervent

Revd Gilespie monument.

denouncing of bishops in Scotland, Archbishop Sharp ordered his headstone be taken to the mercat cross and broken up by the town's common hangman in 1661. In 1746, his grandson, also George Gillespie, minister at Strathmiglo, had a new memorial erected. In 1808, the church was remodelled and made larger, which resulted in Revd George Gillespie ending up buried within the church walls. His memorial now sits in the church porch and the site of his grave is in front of the stained-glass window dedicated to him and Covenanter Alexander Henderson.

The kirkyard is host to many fascinating graves that tell a wider story of the town. These include a remarkable stone to the Oliphant-Alison shipowning family, who proudly display one of the best gravestones for a Freemason seen in fife. The east side shows the set square, dividers and triangle, and although there appear to be other tools, the addition of the sun and moon dispel any further argument of it being a trade stone. Another stone that warrants a double take is the soot-blackened sandstone headstone featuring an upturned boat with two figures on top: 'Andrew Henderson in memory of his brother David lost at sea 1808.'

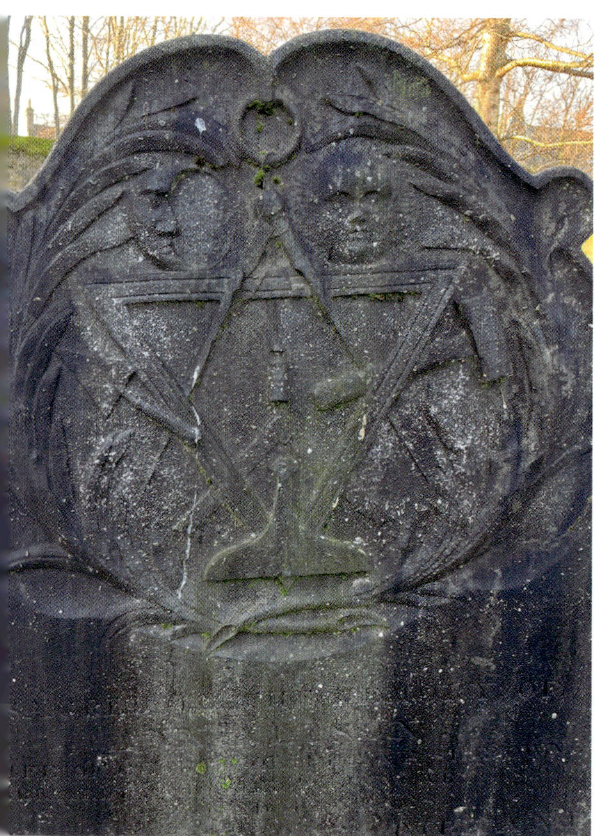

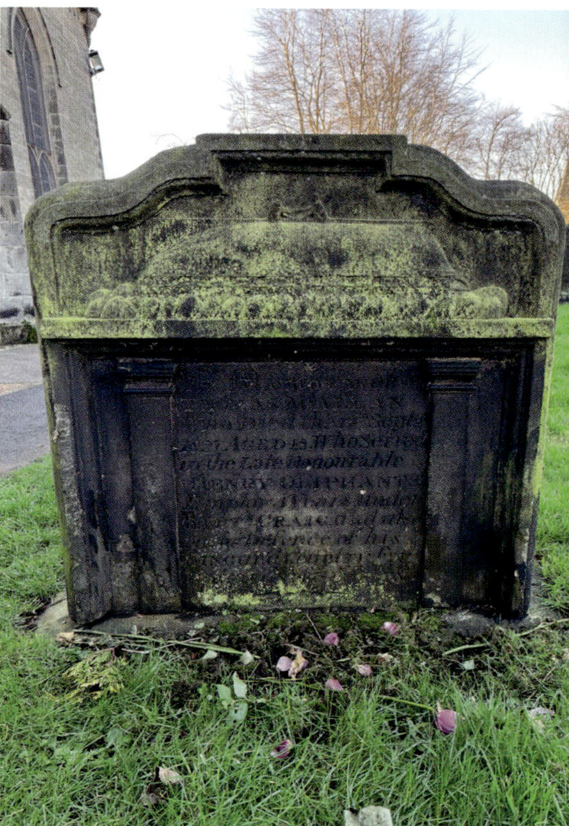

Above left: Freemason gravestone.

Above right: Upturned boat carving.

Abbotshall Parish Church, Abbotshall Road, Kirkcaldy, KY2 5PH
There is a real mixture of graves here, with the earliest dating from 1658 (eight years after the establishment of the parish and its church) right through to the twenty-first century with interments still taking place. This has resulted in there being many headstones of different centuries nestled together. It is a graveyard that seems to naturally inspire exploration of the gravestones off the pathways. In fact, to see some of the more interesting ones you have to make your way through the grass-covered areas to the rear of the church building. It is here that you will find the likes of the red sandstone grave of William Taylor, a stunning piece of craftsmanship, and it is far from surprising that the 'stone carver of this town' would have such a memorial. The trend of having one's trade carved on a headstone lost its popularity in the early nineteenth century, simple moulded markers conveying a trade in its epitaph taking precedence. This stone is truly beautiful; the detail is exquisite. Purposely unfinished and leaving a rustic exterior, the mell's handle is broken off as if to signify the work is finished before its time. The top two sections for William and his wife Susan seem to have been done in a different hand so it may be assumed William created the body of it himself in life. This stone not only captivates the eye but also the mind.

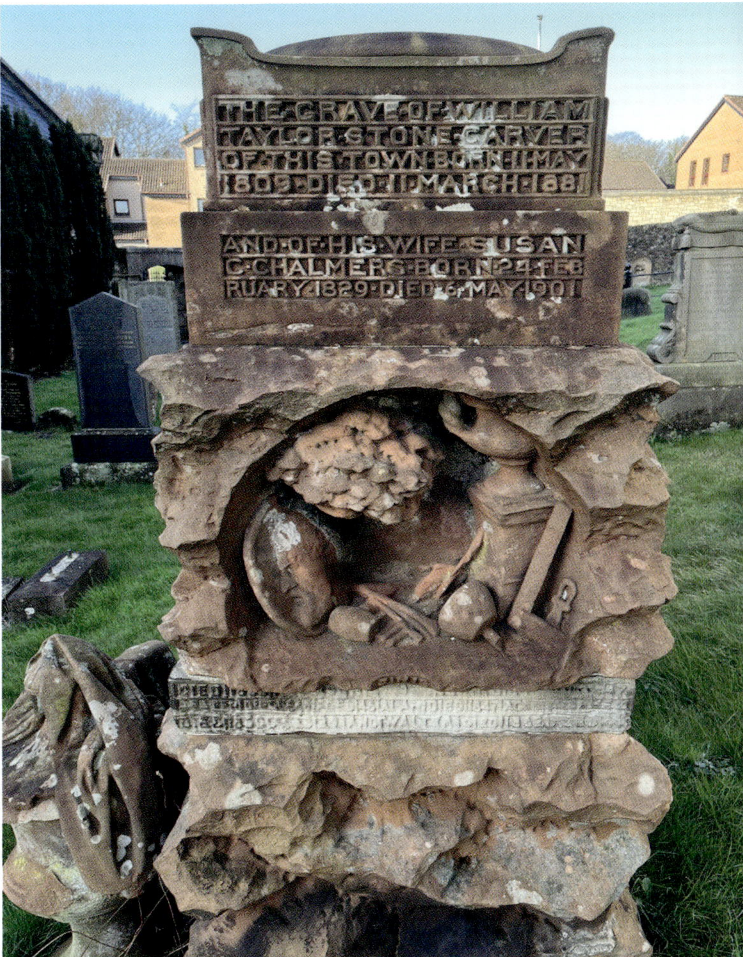

William Tailor's gravestone.

From one master stone carver to another. This carving was created by the celebrated Pinkington Jackson, whose most famous commission is the mounted statue of Robert the Bruce that forms the focal point of the memorial for the Battle of Bannockburn. The grave of Marjory Fleming (13 January 1803 – 19 December 1811) gained this sculpture by Jackson in 1930. 'Pet Marjorie', as she is also referred to, has been credited as 'The Youngest Immortal in the World of Letters'. A child diarist who is best remembered for a diary she kept in the last eighteen months of her life before contracting what is now believed to be meningitis a month short of her ninth birthday. For fifty years after her death they remained private; however, during the Victorian period they were finally published, though early editions were reworked and edited as some of the language she used was deemed inappropriate for an eight-year-old. She gained literary admiration from Robert Louis Stevenson, who was quoted on a dust jacket: 'Marjory Fleming was possibly – no, I take back possibly – she was one of the noblest works of God.' While Mark Twain commented, 'She was made out of thunderstorms and sunshine.' Her manuscripts and writings are now kept in the National Library of Scotland with the digitalised scans being available to the public.

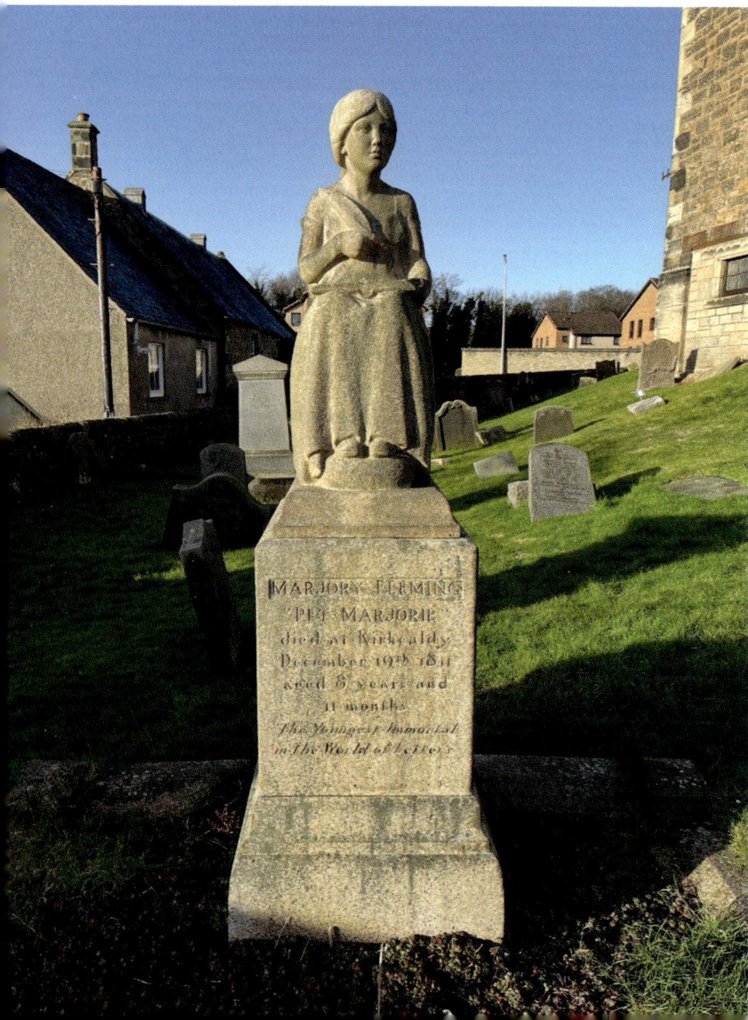

Pet Marjory.

Leslie

Christ's Kirk on the Green, Greenside, KY6 3ED
Fife is not a place you instantly recall when you think of the *Titanic*; however, there is a notable *Titanic* survivor whose final resting place is in Leslie. Lucy Noël Martha Dyer Edwards was born on 25 December 1878, though she adopted her middle name as her chosen name and is often reported in the newspaper articles of the early twentieth century as Noëlle. A beauty of society, she was much sought after and on 19 April 1900 she married Norman Leslie, the 19th Earl of Rothes, becoming the Countess of Rothes. In 1904, they took up residence at Leslie House in Leslie and the countess became involved in many charitable causes in Scotland, especially in the local area. She established a branch of the Red Cross and endowed it with three ambulances, which in turn led to a larger ambulance corps serving Fife. She also established the Countess of Rothes Voluntary Aid Detachment. She held the community very dear and every Christmas, though not celebrated in Scotland at this time, on her birthday she would have entertainment put on at the village hall and treated all the children to a gift. It is because of this she was given the affectionate nickname 'the Christmas Countess'.

When the *Titanic* struck the iceberg on that fateful night of 14 April, the countess, travelling with a relative and maid, had already retired for the night; yet, at 1 a.m. they were all on lifeboat 8, the first lifeboat to be lowered on the port side. With mostly women on board, able-bodied seaman Thomas William Jones took charge; however, it wasn't long before the countess took the tiller, ordering the women to row. She was one of those who voiced their opinion that they should return after the *Titanic* sank to look for survivors, but was overwhelmingly outnumbered by the frightened women who feared the boat would be swamped. In the subsequent enquiries Jones would go on to described her as 'More of a man than any we had on board'. This gained her a new nickname, given by the newspapers – 'the Plucky Little Countess'. The countess and Jones would hold each other in great esteem. Jones had the '8' from the lifeboat framed and gave it to her as a keepsake, while she gifted him a silver pocket watch, and the two continued a lifelong correspondence until the countess's death.

When the earl died in 1927 he was laid to rest in the Leslie mausoleum. The countess went on to marry Colonel Claud Macfie. Understandably, it would seem she never lost her love of the little Fife village and its people. When she died in Hove, Sussex, on 12 September 1956, many assumed she was buried there. However, it has since been discovered that after her cremation at Downs Crematorium, Brighton, her ashes were buried next to her first husband at the Leslie side of the twin-gabled burial vault, while Colonel Macfie had his scattered at sea by his stepson Malcolm George Dyer-Edwards, as per his wishes. There is a memorial to her at St Mary's Church in Fairford, put in place in 1957, but only after Colonel Macfie was able to persuade the minister who said there would be no more memorials in the church after paying for the laying of paving slabs around

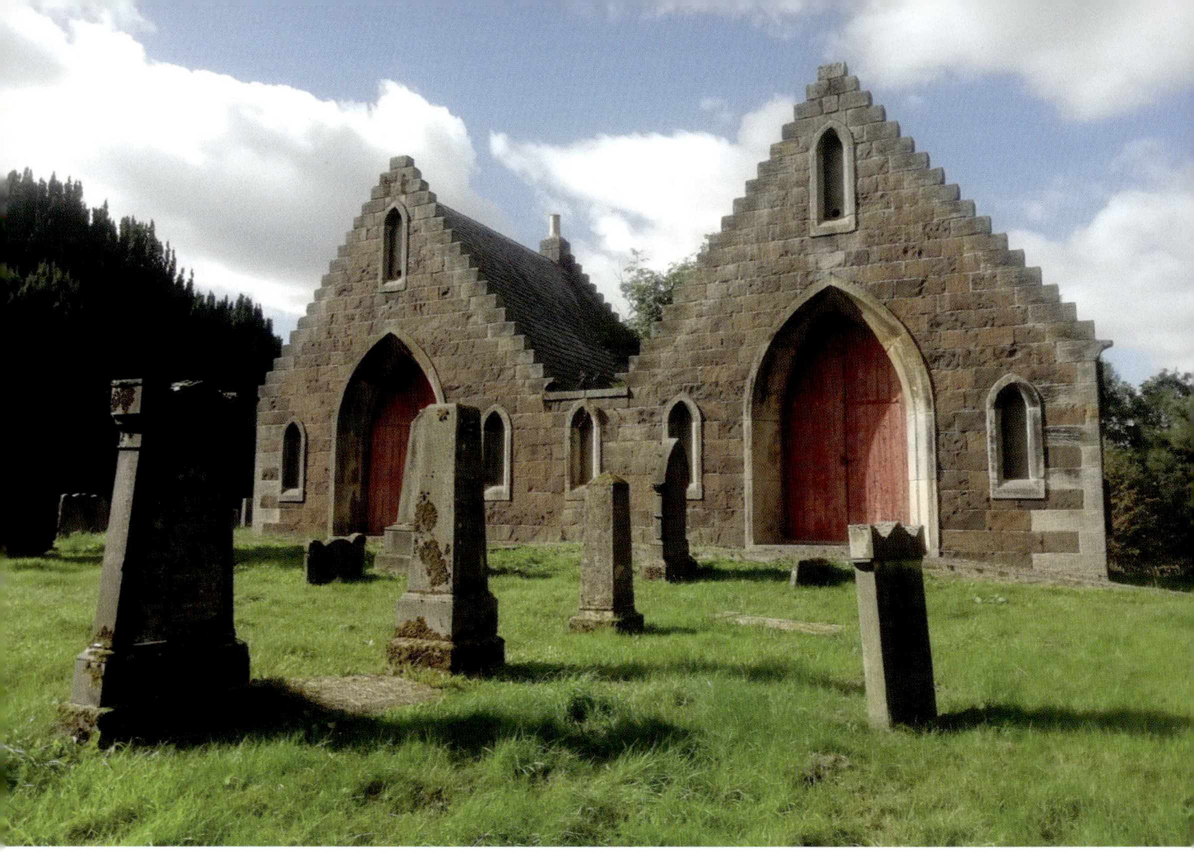

Rothes Mausoleum is to the right.

the church from the nearby demolished Fairfieldpark House. The white and gold monument proudly displays the Rothes coat of arms and declares: 'Noëlle, widow of the 19th Earl of Rothes and beloved wife of Col Claude Macfie D.S.O. of Fayre Court, Fairford. At rest 12 Sept 1956.'

Christ's Kirk on the Green Church was converted into residential use in 1994, though the graveyard to the rear can still be accessed through the pretty lychgate. While the site has been used for worship since medieval times the majority of the church building is from the nineteenth century. Many of the grave markers predate this, however, and there is a lovely selection dating from the seventeenth century that justifies seeking out this tucked-away burial ground. On the green to the front there is a curious stone that grabs attention and, while not a burial stone, warrants an explanation.

The Bull Stone is a relic from an era where groups such as the chapmen would meet on the green for both sport and recreation. The blood sport of bull-baiting was practised here, but was eventually banned with the passing of the Cruelty to Animals Act of 1835. The unusual shape is due to the wearing away of the granite caused by the rope or chain tethering the animal. Not only was this considered a source of entertainment, but there was a wide-held belief that bull-baiting caused the meat to be tenderised and was therefore better for consumption. It was categorised as a Class C listed building at the same time the church was converted.

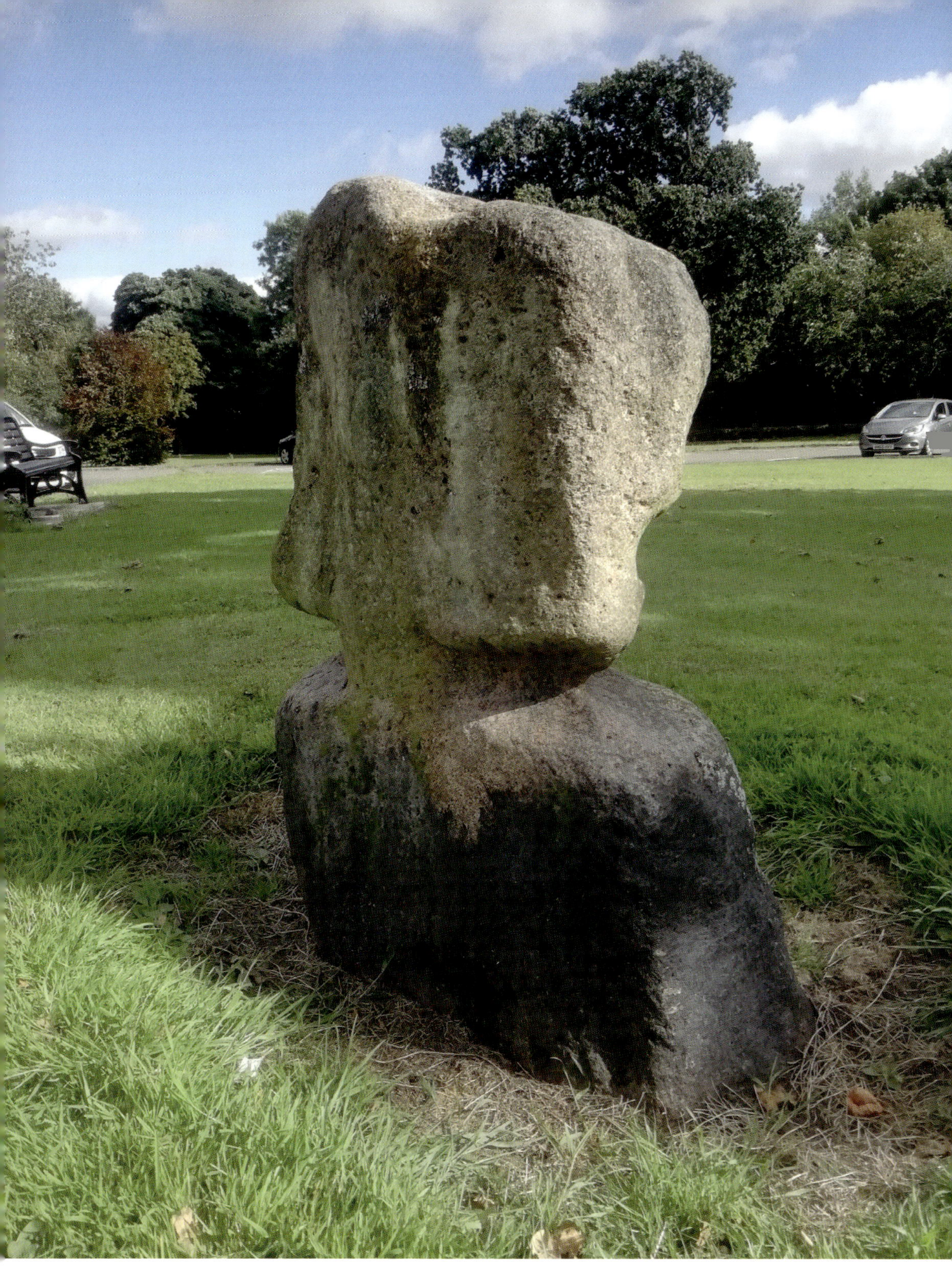

Bull Stone.

6

The District of Cupar

Established in 1591, the presbytery of Cupar was the least populated of the four; however, what it lacks in population it certainly makes up for in the richness of interesting burial grounds. Made up from parishes along the River Tay to its north and including hilly areas such the Lomond Hills towards central Fife, agriculture was the main source of employment for many years, though handloom weaving was an industry that was taken up by many in the more rural areas. It was an area once favoured by royalty for leisure, not only with Falkland Palace, a royal hunting lodge, but the 'healing airs' at Balmerino. While there was a seafaring community, it was to a lesser degree than the southern parts of Fife. Here, life on the water was more for pleasure, transport or training.

Falkland

Falkland Old Kirkyard, High Street, KY15 7BU
Falkland has enjoyed royal patronage in the past, but has stayed snugly tucked away from much of the modern world in central Fife until very recent times when it featured in the filming of *Outlander*, standing in as Inverness when its charm and character captivated audiences all over the world. Moving away from the pretty square, with the Bruce Fountain at its ornamental centre, and along the High Street to Kilgour Old Burial Ground (also known as the Falkland Old Parish Kirkyard) we discover the people who called this area home centuries ago. Here are some exceptional examples of trade gravestones that have stood the test of time – perhaps in part due to being away from industrial pollution and being in a reasonably sheltered location.

There are two trade stones that stand out from many others in their professions. The first is perhaps the most photographed within Falkland and clearly belongs to a cooper. Its central, uppermost carving is the immortality symbol of the winged soul. Its face is soft featured and almost cartoon in style. There is nothing sinister or frightening about the message it gives us as even the skulls, there to remind us that death comes to us all, do not seem particularly threatening – they are reminiscent of Boni from *Trap Door* (people of a certain age will understand the reference!).

The other grave that should be highlighted is that of Charles Honyman, a weaver of the parish, and his wife Isabel. Much of the writing has eroded away

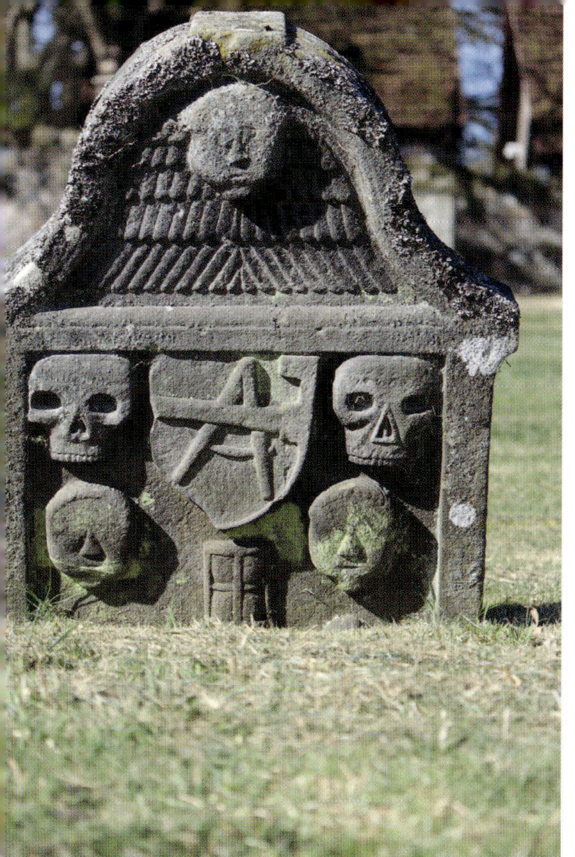 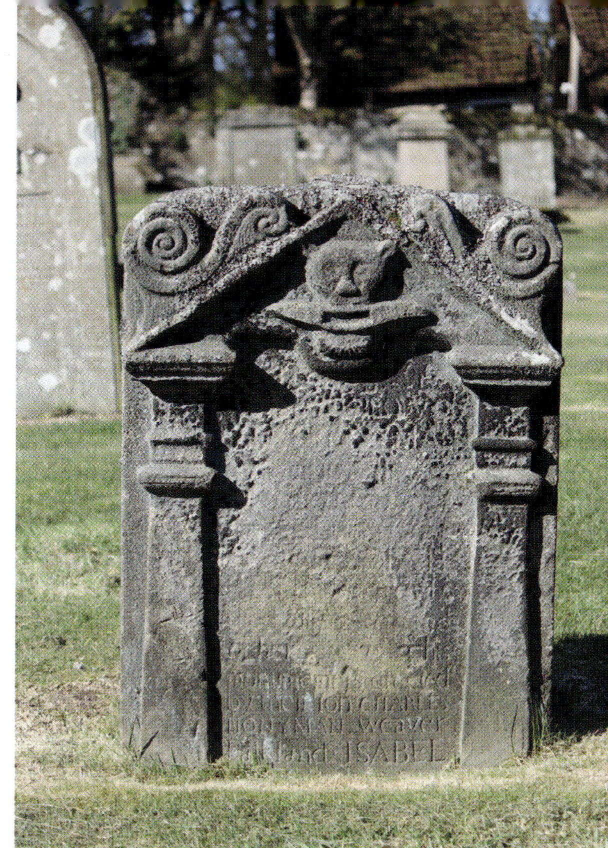

Above left: Cooper's grave.

Above right: Weaver's grave featuring leopard insignia.

and in coming decades the names too shall fade. However, the trade emblem, one of the most noteworthy weavers' stones in Fife, will carry the message of who is buried there by his profession. Proudly centred as the main feature of the stone is the leopard's head with a mighty shuttle in its mouth. This is the stone of someone who took immense pride in his profession.

Auchtermuchty

Edenshead Parish Church – Auchtermuchty, High Street, Auchtermuchty, KY14 7AP
Auchtermuchy's past is as interesting as its name. Once home to many wild boar, the Pictish settlement was called Uachdar Mucadidh, which translates to 'upland of the boar'. The Romans established a temporary camp here, which has been dated to around AD 210, while an archaeological dig in 1988 found artifacts to suggest that medieval dwellers of the area later used the Roman trenches as rubbish dumps. The current church building dates from 1779; however, it is evident from the age of some of the gravestones, dating from the late seventeenth century, that the burial ground is older and a previous church building once stood here. There

was a church granted to Lindores Abbey at Auchtermuchty in 1350, but there is no record of where it stood exactly. The range of stones and interesting carvings are worth taking time to study and examine – they've evidently been carved with different levels of skill. It should also be noted that this is a churchyard that is particularly beneficial to visit in the morning if photography is important.

The most curious of the gravestones is carved with an unfinished Green Man as its focal feature, a rather morose expression upon his face. Simply dedicated to 'R.B. and M.R.' with the date '1756', it tells us very little else about who it belonged to. The central area where the symbols of trade may have been is unfinished like various other sections. Most likely it was installed on site, with work being done in the grounds rather than being installed after completion. It is an unusual symbol to find in Fife, so perhaps the owners of the burial marker were not so pleased with the artist's attempts at being a bit different.

There is a flat stone here from 1737 that draws particular attention. Belonging to farmer Andrew Richardson, who seemed to take pride in his work, his epitaph declares: 'A husbandman who ploughed in art, In hope he sowed and in reap did partake, With skill the produce of the Earth improved.' Of all the imagery produced, it's the book and figures of Andrew and his wife that demand a second look. The open book has the words 'I am what I am' and the naked figures seem to have a hint of a smile still detectable – presumably confident of the outcome on the Day of Judgement.

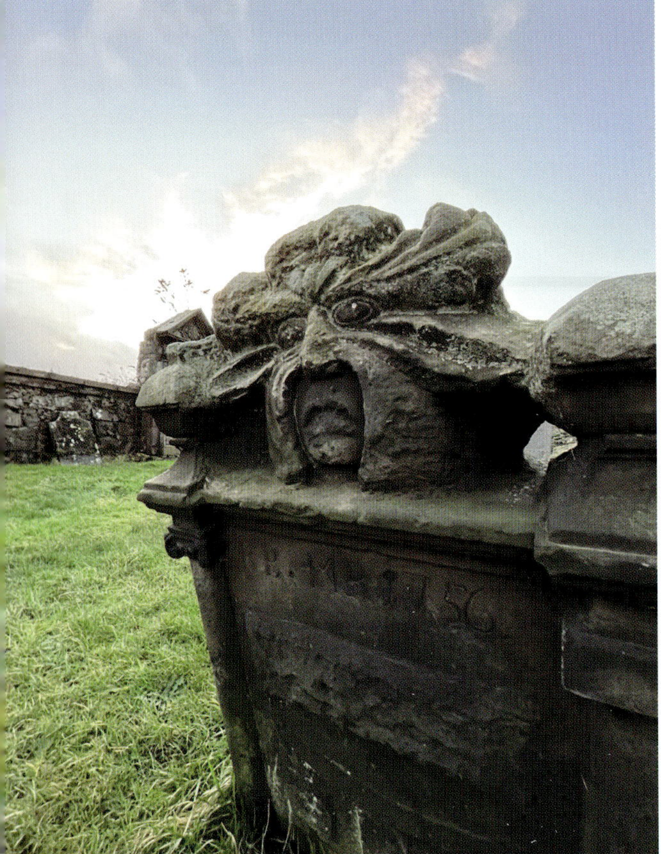

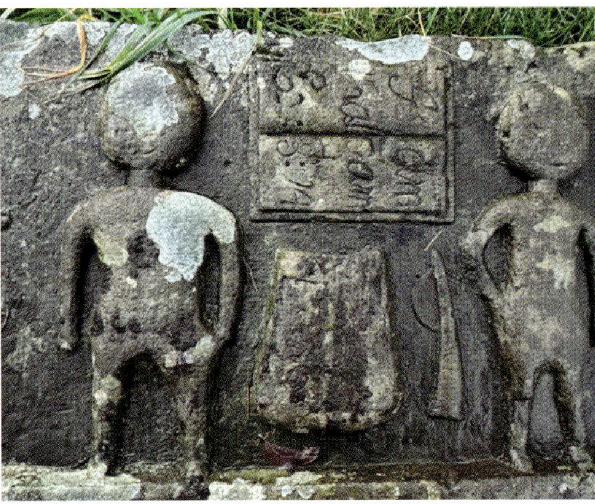

Above: Farmer's flat stone detail.

Left: Unfinished Green Man carving.

Seemingly out of place among a selection of grave markers from an earlier century is the double-sided gravestone for Joseph Low Anderson interred on 28 April 1880 – four months to the day after he was tragically killed in the Tay Bridge disaster. Only twenty years of age, he had been an apprentice at the *Dundee Courier* newspaper. Described as a promising young man, he was nearing the end of his apprenticeship. Being one of their own, the newspaper covered the story of the recovery of his body near Wick. His was the second to last of the forty-six bodies recovered from the seventy-five believed to have gone into the water. It also reported his funeral, which had been attended by a number of his fellow compositors who carried the coffin. It was described as the largest funeral to be seen in his home village of Auchtermuchty for some years. It was understood that Joseph had got on the train at Cupar on 28 December 1879 after spending the day with friends to arrive back in Dundee in time for the night shift. At 7.13 p.m. the train had approached the bridge amid a terrible storm, with winds estimated to have been around 80 mph. Barely 200 yards onto the bridge and the infrastructure collapsed, taking the train with it. Eyewitnesses described seeing flames like from a comet shooting out from the approximate area of the front of the train. The next morning it was clearly seen that the bridge between piers 29 and 41 were missing. Joseph's father, George, was in Dundee for the inquiry when news came to the *Courier* offices of the recovery of a body. Through clothing description, his watch and three printer's leads found in the pockets of his jacket, they were able to identify Joseph and have him returned most solemnly to Dundee where a service was held for him before his final journey home to be laid to rest.

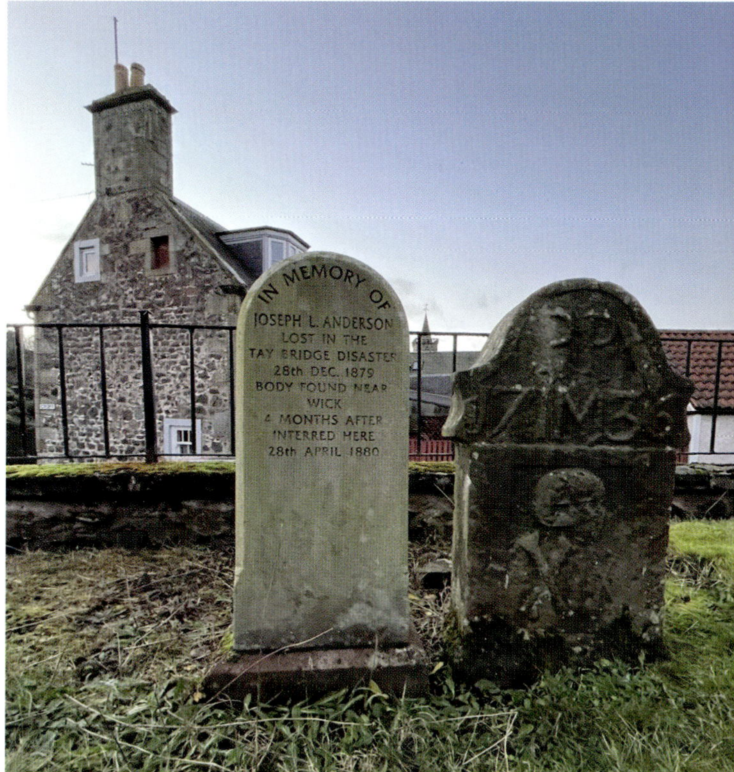

Joseph Anderson – victim of the Tay Bridge disaster.

Cults

Cults Old Parish Church, Kirkton of Cults, KY15 5RD
One of the most tranquil and picturesque hamlet kirkyards in Fife has to be that of Cults Kirk in Kirkton of Cults. Situated up a little lane around a mile from the village of Pitlessie, you pass by the little session house that predates the current church and into a beautiful green space – in the summer the only sounds are from the birds, bees and a little burn nearby. There has been a church on this site since the twelfth century, although the current building was built in 1793. The church bell does tell of an earlier period inscribed with the wording 'John Meikle, Edinburgh fecit for the Kirk of Cults 1699'. As of June 2020, the Kirk of Cults went up for sale. The ancient graveyard and adjoining newer burial ground are owned and maintained by Fife Council. Burials still take place, so visiting the site will never be a problem. There are a number of interesting stones that have been carved with symbols of mortality and they are well worth a visit, especially if you're in the area. A real treasure of a once magnificent mausoleum, all less than a mile north-east from the kirk.

Cults Parish Church.

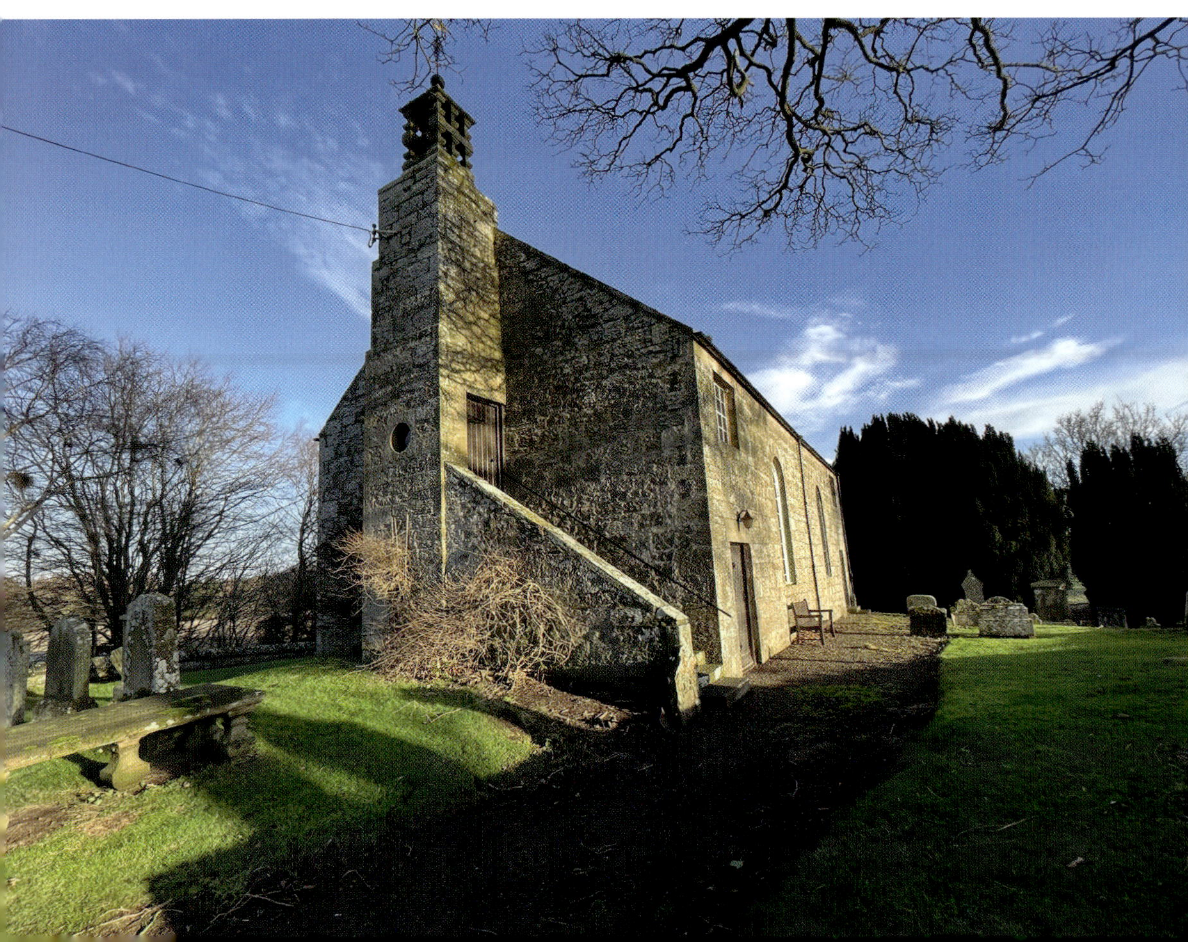

The Crawford family mausoleum is situated in the locally known Lady Mary's Woods on Walton Hill, built inside the remains of an Iron Age fort. While nature has reclaimed the fort structure for the most part, on the west side the lines of the rampart and the ditch can be made out. The mausoleum, built around 1758, is also losing a battle with nature. The once fine Roman Doric columns of this classically designed cruciform-plan mausoleum are crumbling away and, though a category B listed building, it is on the Buildings at Risk Register. Much vegetation now covers it, as well as a couple of well-established trees; however, the third person to be interred here may have just approved of this reclamation of nature.

The first person to be laid to rest inside the great mausoleum was George, 21st Earl of Crawford, after his death on 11 August 1781. Following him was his last remaining son, Major General George Lindsay Crawford, 22nd Earl of Crawford, Lord Lieutenant of Fife and last of the direct male line, who died on 30 January 1808 – a day shy of his fiftieth birthday. His sister, Lady Mary Lindsay Crawford, became the heiress of the family estates. Described as eccentric by many, she had a forthright manner and was reputed to be a most handsome woman into her advanced years. Described as haughty to those who didn't agree with her point of view, she was also considerably loyal and kind to many of the estate workers and servants, many of whom stayed with her for many years. With the family wealth she rebuilt Crawford Lodge as Crawford Priory and surrounded herself with a variety of animals, including a multitude of dogs and birds, a tame fox, a roe deer and her brother's horse, which was to outlive her. In her will she left strict instructions that her heir was to ensure no suffering should come to the horse in any way and how the animal should be put to sleep should the need arise. Her other animals were not to go to 'cruel or barbarous masters'. There is still a touching tribute to her animal companions visible to the rear of the building: a crumbling gravestone dedicated to her brother's favourite roe deer.

whom he daily fed
who followed him home and
slept at his feet.

Upon her death newspapers across the breadth of the country reported on her funeral, which took place on 2 December 1833, a quarter of a century after her brother's. Attended by her closest yet still distant relation the Earl of Glasgow, and many great gentlemen of Fife, an Episcopalian funeral service was held in the Gothic hall of Crawford Priory before the funeral procession made its way up Walton Hill to the mausoleum. Along its route were many of the tenants and townsfolk of Cupar and Ceres come to pay their final respects. A line from the paper, quite sentimental compared to the usual reporting of the death of a person of note reads: 'The gratitude and affection with which it is pleasing to find her memory regarded by those who had the opportunity to know her, will long, we trust be cherished among all classes of her native county.'

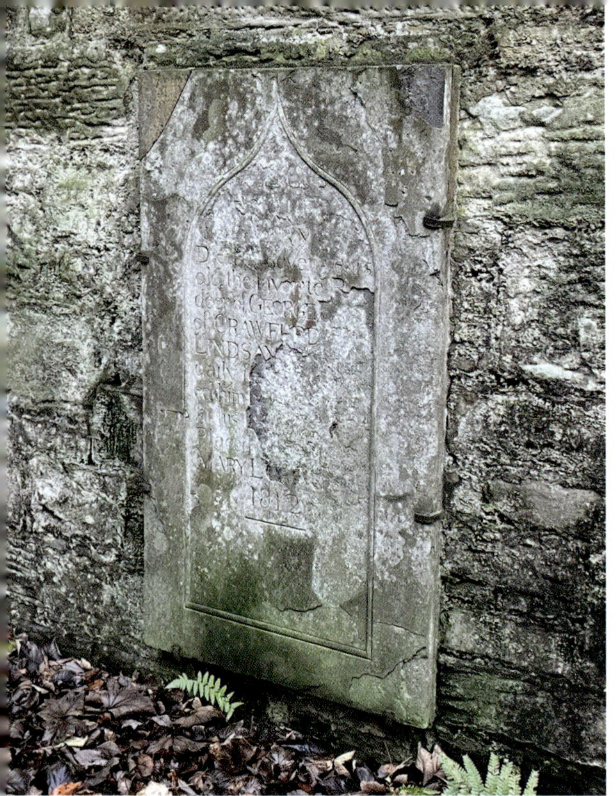

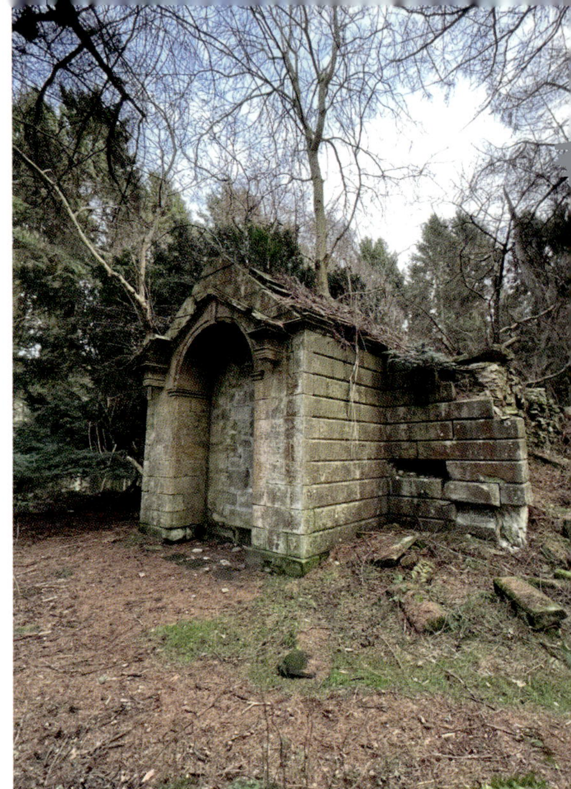

Above left: Deer grave at Crawford Priory.

Above right: Crawford Mausoleum.

Dairsie Old Parish Church, Dairsie, KY15 4RL

Dairsie Old Parish Church is located in a particularly pretty spot, sharing the brow of the hill with Dairsie Castle while overlooking the Dairsie Bridge. The location is a landscape artist's dream, which surprisingly has not yet been painted by any artists of note. The church ceased to be used for worship in 1966 and

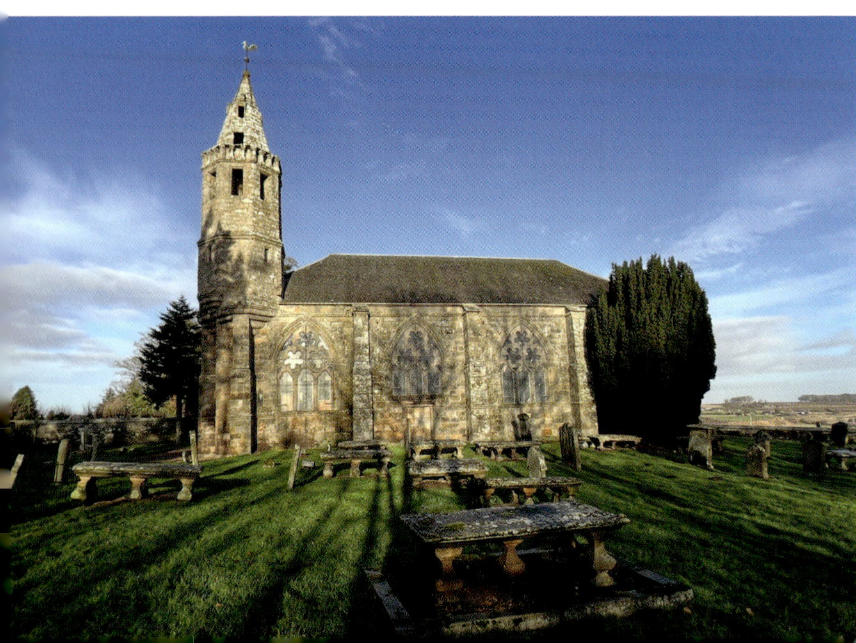

Dairsie Old Parish Church.

it eventually was passed into private ownership. The graveyard and subsequent cemetery has been used since the seventeenth century and boasts some beautiful examples of markers. The church building, for the most part Gothic but with Renaissance features, really is the centrepiece of the grounds. Known formerly as St Mary's, it was built on the instruction of Archbishop Spottiswood who was residing in Dairsie Castle in 1621 and holds the title of being one of Scotland's earliest post-Reformation church buildings. Above the doorway a panel can be seen that contains Spottiswood's arms along with his initials and the words 'IEHOVAH DILEXI DE COREM DOMVS TVAE' translating as 'Jehovah, I have loved the beauty of thy house'.

Cupar

The Parish Church of Cupar Old and St Michael of Tarvit, Kirkgate, KY15 5AL
Edinburgh is often the place most associated with the Covenanters, not only due to the National Covenant being first signed within the walls of Greyfriars Kirk in 1638 but also due to the publicised trials, executions and of course the imprisonment of many in the Covenanters' Prison after the Battle of Bothwell Bridge on 22 June 1679. Even today many from across the world make their way to Greyfriars to visit the Martyrs' Monument. However, what people may not realise is that northern Fife was a concentrated area for the Covenanter movement, and with it came their own martyrs. Here at Cupar is a grave for three such men, or at least part of them. The Covenanter's Grave is a short way into the grounds and accessed by the single gate at the rear wall. It is not hard to miss and the symbology on it is far from subtle. Across the top are two disembodied heads

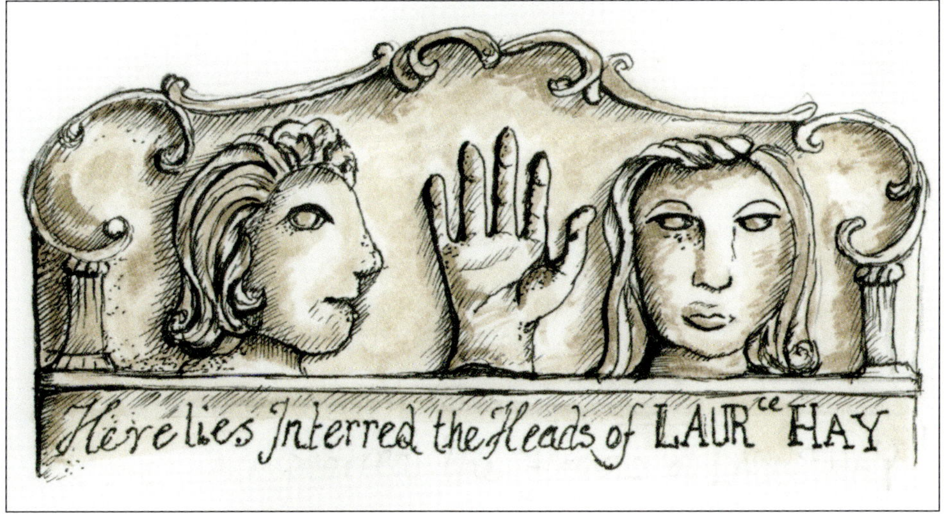

Covenanter's stone detail.

and a lone right hand at its centre. This is the first indicator of the body parts that lie interred below the ground. The front of the stone reads:

> Here lie interred the Heads of LAURce HAY
> and ANDREW PITULLOCH who
> suffered martyrdom at EDINr. July 13th 1681
> for adhering to the word of GOD & Scotland
> covenanted work and Reformation and also
> one of the hands of DAVID HACKSTON
> of Rathillot who was most cruelly murdered
> at EDINr. July 30th 1680
> for the same cause.

David Hackston's part in the assassination of Archbishop James Sharp has always been questionable, so for now the focus will be on his death. After the assassination, far from going into hiding he took part in drawing up and publishing *The Declaration and Testimony of the True Presbyterian Party in Scotland*, a piece that condemned the government's meddling in Scottish religious affairs. He then went on to fight at both the Battle of Drumclog on 1 June 1679 and then the Battle of Bothwell Bridge three weeks later on 22 June. Unlike many of his fellow Covenanters, he evaded capture and a reward was placed on his head. He was eventually captured at Airds Moss in Ayrshire where he was badly wounded in a skirmish and taken to Edinburgh. He was then sentenced to the barbaric execution of being hanged, drawn and quartered, and his hands were to be struck from his body afterwards. His body parts were distributed around the country to serve as a reminder to the populous. His right hand went to Cupar where it was buried.

Laurence Hay and Andrew Pitulloch, or Pitullo as he is also referred, were members of an illegal open-air society for prayer and conference. In 1680, the privy council issued a proclamation stating that such field meetings were 'rendezvouses of rebellion'. Hay and Pitullo went further than others and put their signatures to a paper entitled 'A Testemony Against the Evils of the Times'. For this they were executed at the Grassmarket in Edinburgh on 13 July 1681 by hanging. Once dead, their heads were removed and affixed to the tollbooth in Cupar, where they were to stay until 1689. With the re-establishment of a full Presbytery church in Scotland once more, their heads were removed and buried alongside Hackston's hand.

The ancient burial ground has quite a selection of newer stone, with the more time-weathered pieces sporadically dotted in between. One 'stone' of particular note is a cast-iron marker from the nineteenth century. Many cast-iron grave markers found in Scottish burial grounds have either eroded to such a degree that they are illegible or have disappeared by human hand all together. This, however, is an exceedingly fine example belonging to Robert Davidson, a civil engineer born in Cupar on 20 October 1782, but who spent most of his life in Paris as an

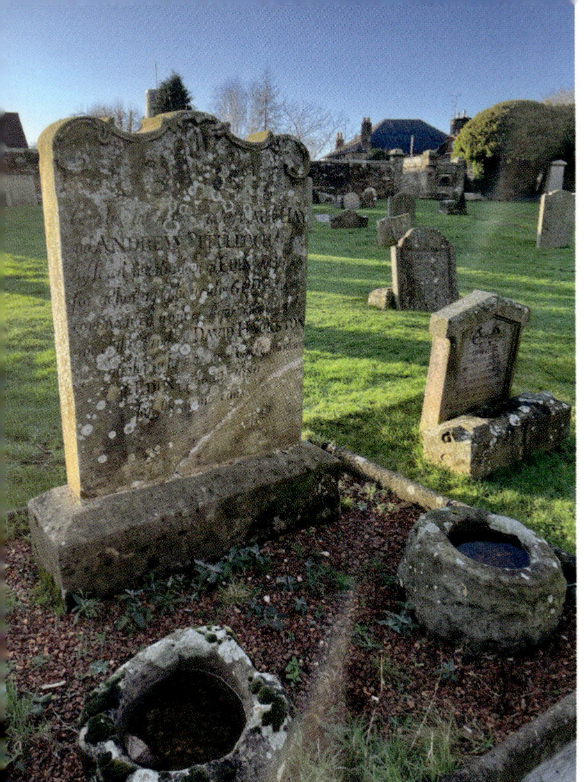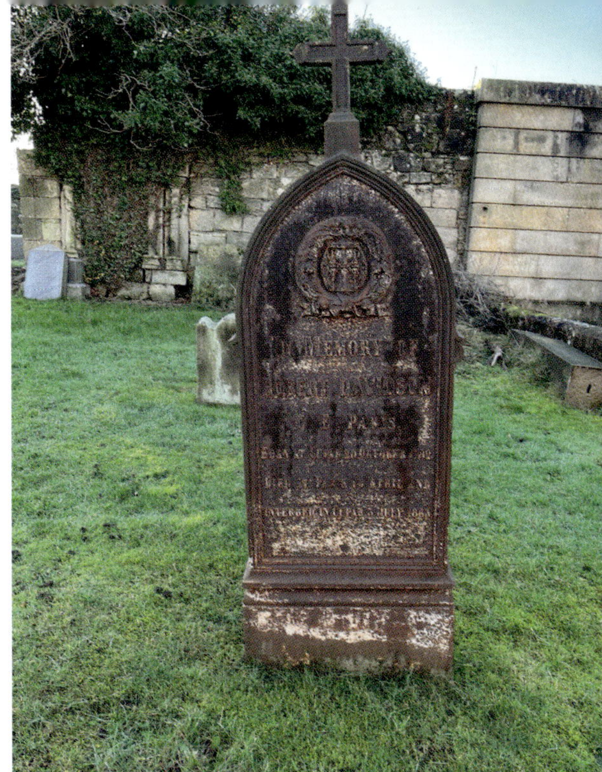

Above left: Covenanter's stone.

Above right: Iron grave marker of Robert Davidson.

ironfounder. He died in his adopted French city on 14 April 1863 at the advanced age of eighty-one and was interred in Cupar on 3 July of the same year, with his burial marker coming from his own foundry – seen on the lower right. He died unmarried and without a will, so his fortune, which today would amount to around £3.5 million, was distributed between his four surviving siblings and the families of those who predeceased him. As one local newspaper, a little snootily, declared: 'They all belong to the working classes … and the death of their wealthy relative places them in comparative affluence.'

Abdie

At Abdie, before even entering the grounds of the kirkyard, there are two curious buildings dedicated to the protection of the dead: to the left is a watch house and to the right is a mort house. Although not particularly near the coast of the River Tay, the good people of this parish, it would seem, were particularly fearful of the resurrectionist threat. This theory is further backed by the evidence that the kirk ruins were turned into a giant mort safe with bars installed in the windows and heavy-duty doors installed once more.

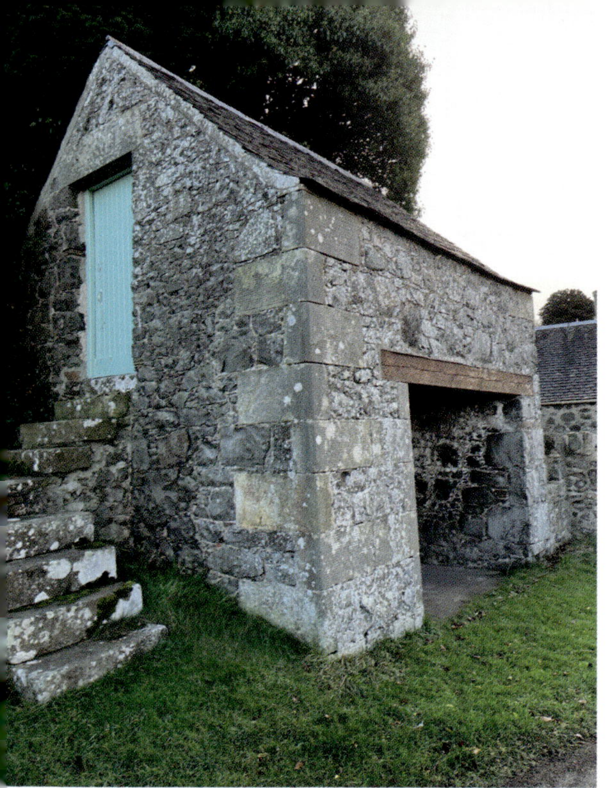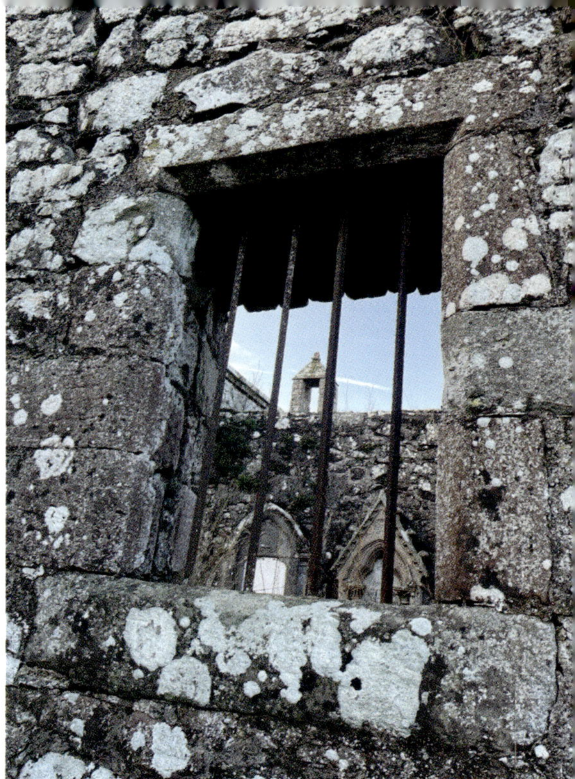

Above left: Abdie Mort House.

Above right: Barred windows on the kirk ruin.

The mort house is now home to a fascinating Pictish stone, the Lindores Stone, which is now sheltered from the elements. The first recorded discovery was in 1830 when it was seen lying on its side on Kaim Hill above Lindores. Within the next couple of decades it moved and was built into a stone wall in the village where it would stay for over a hundred years. There are conflicting reports, both academic and local observations, of when it was moved exactly but it is generally agreed to have been 1970. On closer inspection it is evident that it was employed as a sundial, with markings relatively recent in comparison to the fine example of Pictish symbolism. There is also an even more recent three-pronged benchmark symbol. The earliest markings date from the seventh century and comprise of the crescent and its V rod, which instantly draw the eye; however, the triple disc or cauldron symbol above and the mirror on the right-hand side are equally noteworthy, if not as decorative. Unfortunately, most symbol significance from this distant time can only be speculated. The only document to survive was copied in Latin by scribes of a later era – a list of their kings. Perhaps today we should be grateful that the worst this stone suffered was its use being altered, as Scotland has lost many national treasures from the Pictish period in the last few centuries through breaking these types of stone up to build dyke walls and the like.

The burial ground has a mixture of memorials of various dates, though sadly it lacks many of the early markers that would have been here. From evidence of

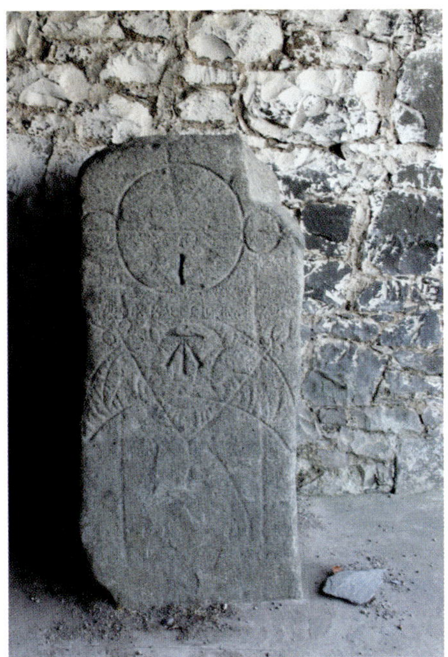

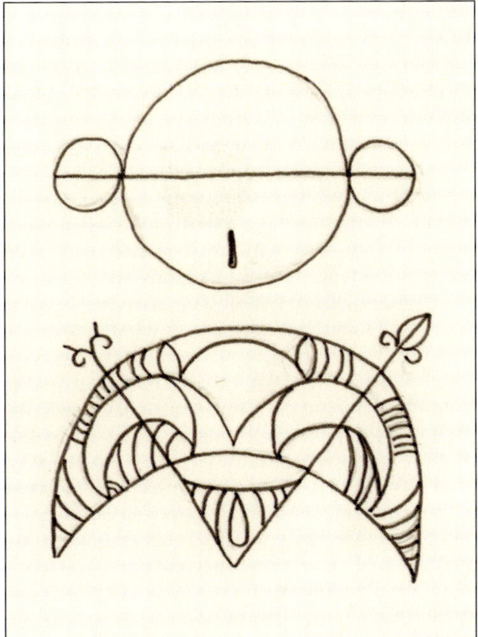

Above left: Lindores Pictish stone.

Above right: Stone detail.

stones no longer in their original setting and being either stacked in a corner or against the rear wall of the kirk, it is likely many have subsequently been buried or repurposed. In an area of much weaving the symbol of the shuttle or loom would be expected to adorn a number of stones, but sadly there are only a handful of trade stones here. Of the families buried here the Maitlands are of particular note. The most famous Maitland is buried in Bombay: Sir Frederick Lewis Maitland, Captain of HMS *Bellerophon* – Napoleon surrendered to him on 15 July 1815, marking the end of the Napoleonic Wars. There is also mention of him in memorials at the new church of Abdie and Dunbog; St Ann's Church, Plymouth; and St Thomas Cathedral, Mumbai. His widow and children are interred here at Abdie, however.

Collessie

Collessie Parish Church, Church Lane, KY15 7RQ
The little village of Collessie is one of Fife's true hidden gems. Once on the principal highway to St Andrews, it now lives sleepily north of the A91. With this bypass the collection of pretty seventeenth- and eighteenth-century cottages in the older part of the village nestled round the thirteenth-century church location at the top of a hillock have remained virtually untouched by modern life. The old

tales that have passed down through the centuries declare that this community of weavers and agricultural workers was often visited by James V (1512–42) when he was staying at Falkland Palace, who favoured the place and its people. James was reputed to wander in various locations in Scotland incognito, declaring himself to be 'The guid man o Ballengeich' – Ballengeich is a steep pass at Stirling Castle used by the king as a secret exit. Coming to the throne at the young age of two, he was curious to know how different life could have been for him had he not been king.

Winding through its twisting lanes and coming to the entrance of Collessie Church, attention is drawn to the outer wall of the Melville of Halhill tomb, its yellow a sharp contrast to the nearby natural stone of the perimeter wall. It was built to house the body of Christian Boswell in 1609 and later her husband Sir James Melville, who was the first person to actually be documented to have been buried in Collessie churchyard. Sir James was the third son of Sir John Melville, Laird of Raith, who was executed for treason in 1548. Months later James was sent to France to become a page for Mary, Queen of Scots. It can be assumed he was a good and faithful servant to her, as when she returned to Scotland in 1561 she bestowed a pension on him and further granted him a position in her household. He went on to serve both Mary and her son James VI, and again it would seem he served his monarch well as he was knighted at the coronation of Anne of Denmark – James's wife. As to his own wife, he married Christian Boswell in 1569 and they had eight children together, several reaching adulthood. He was a believer in education for both boys and girls, so it is little wonder that his daughter Elizabeth Melville, later Lady Culross, would find fame as Scotland's first woman poet to see her writing in print. In 1605, Robert Chatteris issued the first edition of her poem 'Ane Godlie Dreame' in Edinburgh. It has been accredited that the words seen on the tomb are also her work. It is an elaborate example of a type of a now rare righteous public exhortation that

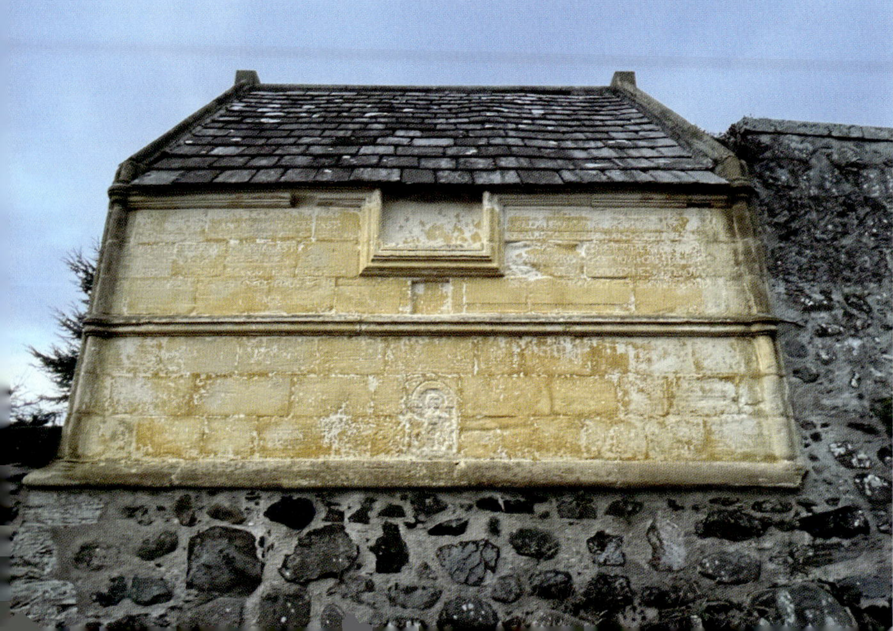

Melville
Mausoleum.

grew in popularity following the Reformation and as such it is of the utmost importance to preserve it.

> Ye loadin pilgrims passing langs this way
> Pans on your fall and your offences past
> How your frail flesh first formit of the clay
> Un dust mon be desolvit at the last
> Resent amend on Christ he burden cast
> Of pour sad sinnes who can your sauls refresh
> Syne rais from grave to gloir your grislie flesh
>
> Defyle not christs kirk with your carion
> A solemne sait for gods service prepard
> For praier preaching and communion
> Your byrial should be in the kirkyard
> On your uprysing set your great regard
> When saull and body joynes with joy to ring
> In Heaven for ay with Christ our head and king

At some point during the scourge of the resurrectionists, the tomb was altered for the intended use as a watch house before this purpose was abandoned and it then fell into disrepair. In 2004, the restoration of the Melville Tomb was organised by the Collessie Community Council and was supported by various charitable organisations.

Monimail

Monimail Old Parish Kirkyard, Monimail, KY15 7RJ
One of the most confusing parts of the adventure to find Monimail Old Parish Kirkyard is that it shares the same postcode as the new parish church, yet they are a little distance from each other. Coming to the attractive James Gillespie Graham-designed church, carry on along the road and enter the little hamlet – the entrance is set off the road to the left of the village green. The gravestone that attracts the most fascination – for its subtle and gentle message of death through its carvings – is just to the right, through the gate. While originally belonging to the Blyth family and dating from 1745, it has been reused and inscribed for a later burial to the rear of the stone where it is easier to see the inscription to Marey Lees, wife of Robert McRobbie, who died in 1818. The rear of the stone shows the trade symbols of a maltman, yet it is the outer edges where the message is being relayed to the visitor. While most people would look to the symbology on the stone from left to right, from birth to death, here the tale starts at old age. The face carved on the left is of an old man: his face wrinkled and his brow heavy, yet

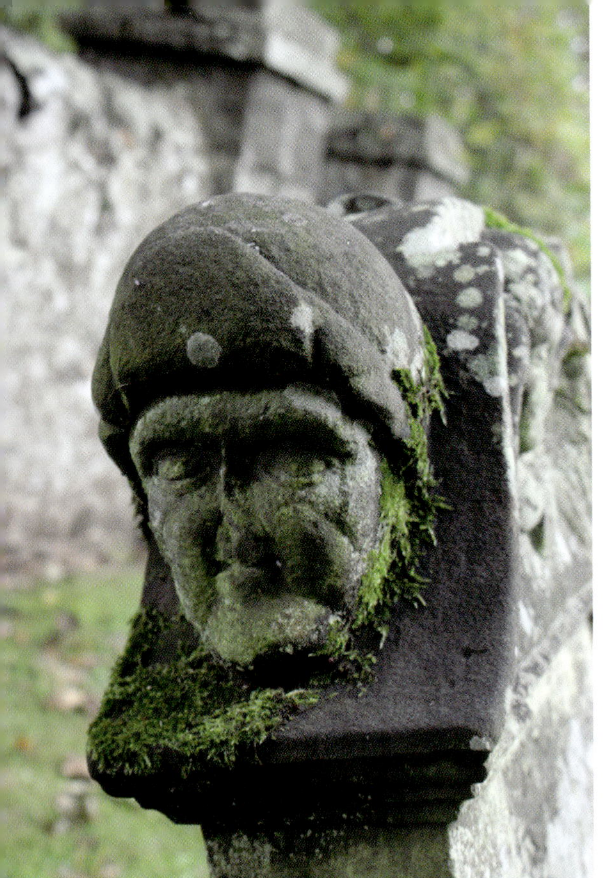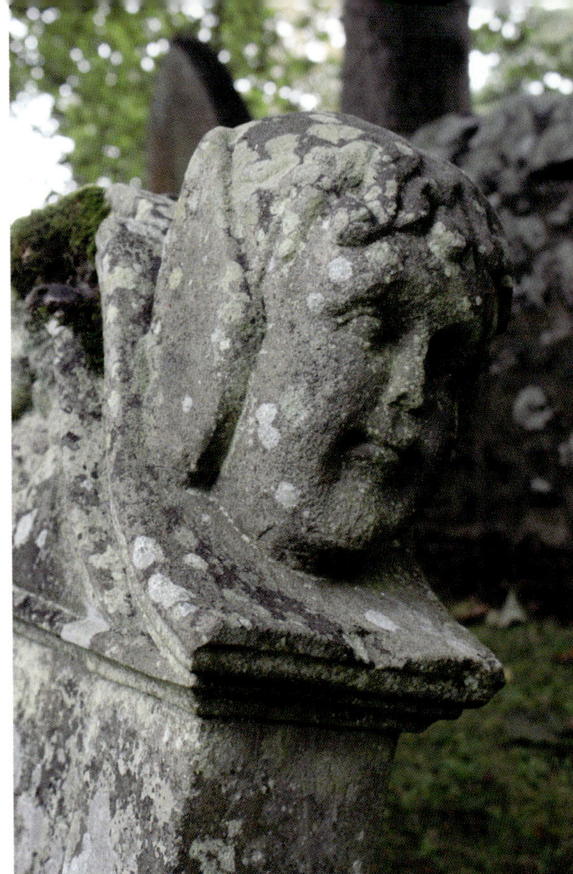

Above left: Elderly carved head – at the end of life.

Above right: Winged soul head – eternally young.

there is a wistful look in his expression, and on his head is a cloth cap to cover his bald head or thinning hair. Moving over the top and the hourglass is on its side, indicating that time been stopped. Coming to the carved face on the right, it is a plump and youthful cherubic face with thick, wavy hair and a pair of wings carved close to the head; this is a representation of the deceased's soul. The tale here is of a man who lived a full and long life that had come to a natural end, but that old, tired body no longer holds the ever-youthful spirit. It is a reminder that death comes to all of us, yet there is no need to grieve as the soul is ever lasting.

Venturing further into the grounds in the southern section is another eighteenth-century stone that commands attention, albeit from a certain angle as gravity has caused it to lean at such a degree it may be overlooked at first glance. It is a carved stone of a husband and wife holding hands as they leave this mortal realm together, dying just a day apart on 26 and 27 March 1750. There is a certain sense that the stonemasons of this era in Monimail possessed a more sensitive approach to depicting death than those employed in some other burial grounds. While there is a skull carving or two to be found within the kirkyard, they do not seem to feature as prominent focal pieces.

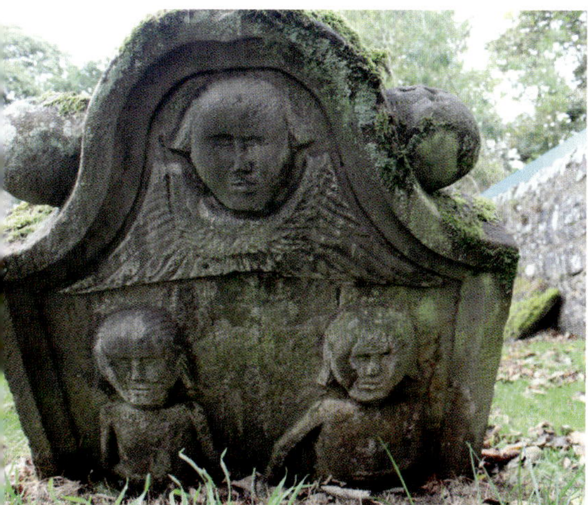 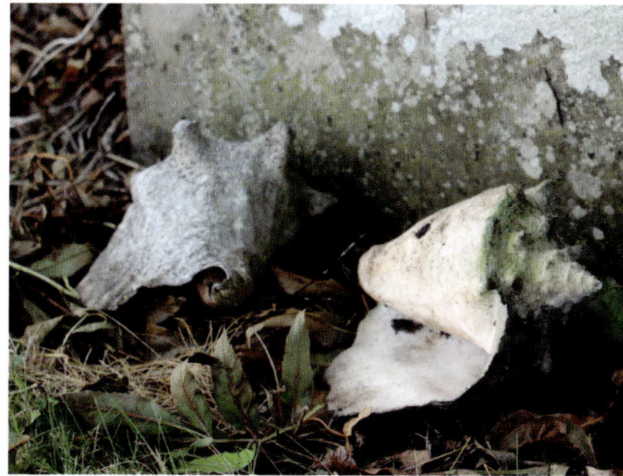

Above left: Husband and wife together forever.

Above right: Conch shells.

There are other features to be found in this little kirkyard that warrant special mention, such as the fragile antique conch shells left by a couple of the grave markers. Conch shells are not native to the cold waters of the British Isles and come from areas such as the Caribbean, the Florida Keys and the Bahamas. Scallop shells are a symbol of pilgrimage and are associated with

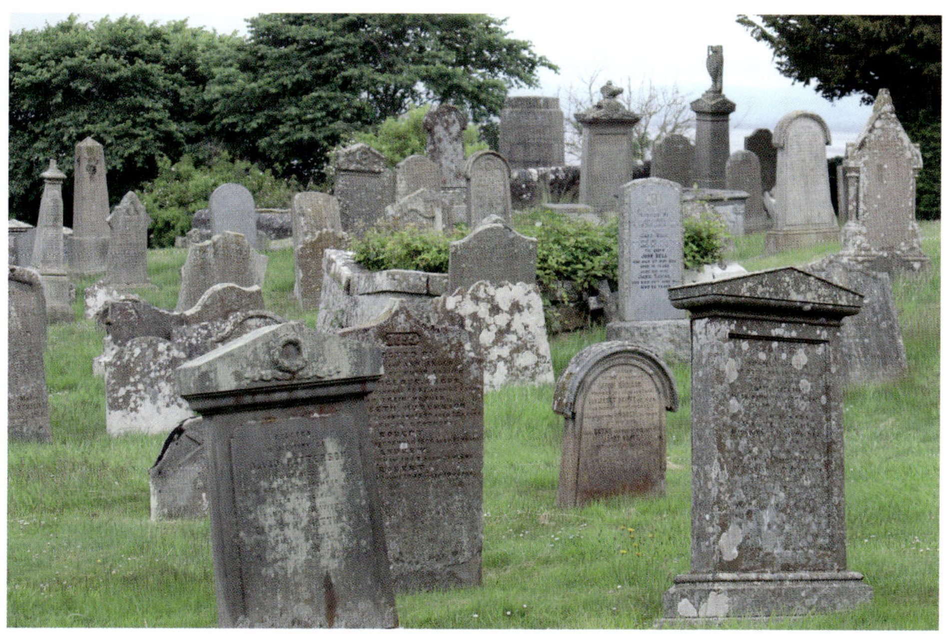

Gravestones at Balmerino.

the Apostle James. Pilgrims would leave them at holy sites to show that they had visited. While the exact meaning of leaving a conch shell has been lost, it is suggested that leaving such an exotic shell symbolised that someone has travelled to visit the departed loved one and show that they have not been forgotten. It was a reminder that lasted longer than flowers and, in some cases, has even lasted longer than the names etched on the accompanying stone. It is also partially a trend of fashion. During the eighteenth and into the nineteenth centuries there was almost a mania for collecting seashells – the more exotic the better.

Balmerino

Balmerino Old Kirkyard connects the road between Balmerino and Kirkton of Balmerino.

The old kirk was built here around 1560 and has burial stones from the sixteenth century – a delightful find. The kirk building was demolished in 1811 and the rubble was used to build up the walls and stairway. It is the central area that has the oldest stones, with the fine monument and enclosures of the Birkhill and Naughton estates at its highest point. It is here that it can be seen how closely

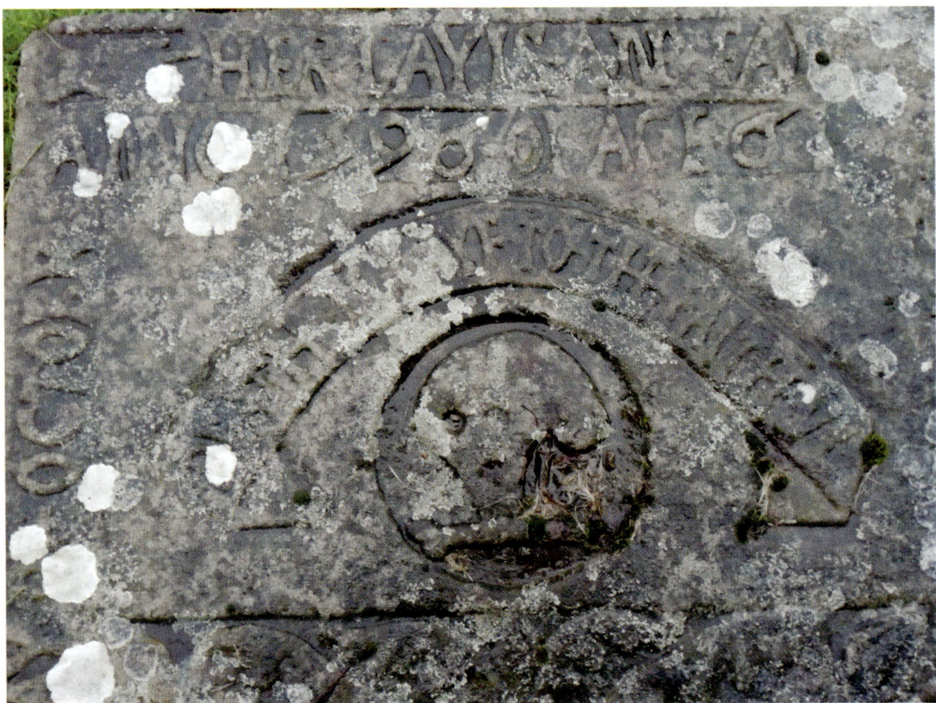

Grave slab, 1596.

the landowners and those who worked the land rest eternally side by side. There is also evidence of dual trade here, as seen with the grave of the local shepherd, his charming crook crossed with the knife of the flesher. This burial ground holds a special place in my heart as it is not only the first one I grew up exploring, but the names on some of the stones from recent decades conjure up loved faces and bring back some happy memories.

The nearby ruins of Balmerino once contained the grave of its founder: Queen Ermingard, widow of William the Lion, who died not long after work began and was buried beneath the high altar. In the 1830s her grave was rediscovered, but unfortunately due to the lack of sensibility of the era her bones were dispersed as curiosities and the soft stone of her white sarcophagus was used by a local Calvanist farmer's wife to sand her kitchen floor. There are three small historic graveyards of the neighbouring parishes of Creich, Flisk, Kilmany all within a reasonable short drive from Balmerino and as such make a fascinating afternoon when visited together.

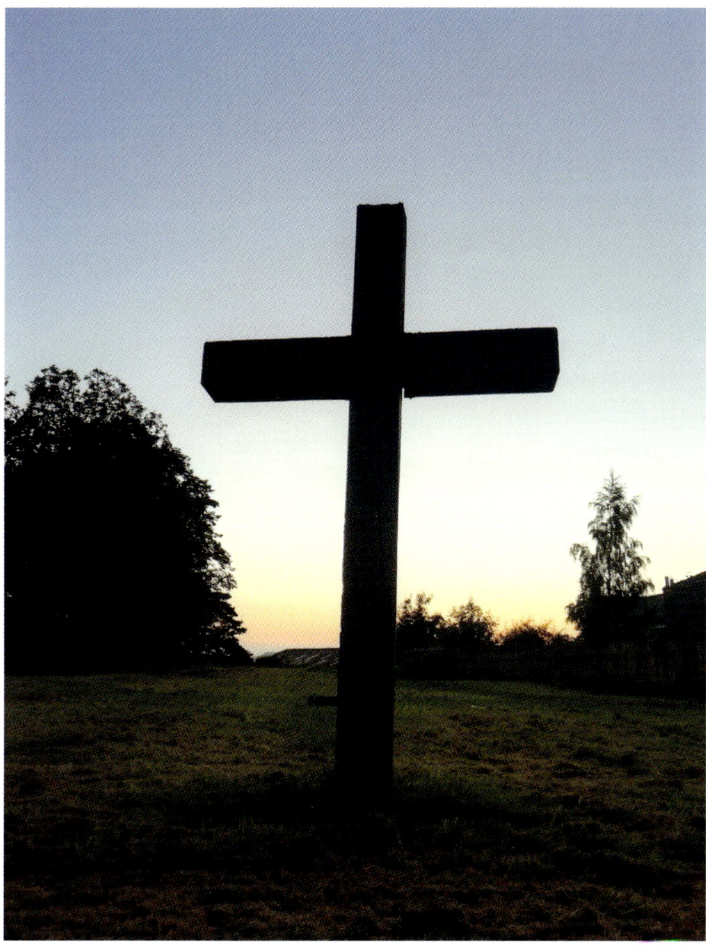

Site of the high altar at Balmerino Abbey.

7

The District of St Andrews

One of the earliest established presbyteries in the whole of Scotland was that of St Andrews, dating from 1587. This was an area that took in the entire east coastline, stretching from the Firth of Forth round to the Firth of Tay. It is an area rich in commerce and education, with Scotland's oldest university situated in St Andrews. Here weavers and fishermen lived beside scholars and ministers.

Largo

Largo Kirk, Church Place, Kirkton of Largo, KY8 6EH
The most curious of gravestones sits in the kirkyard at Upper Largo, or rather the bed of seashells it is nestled in is curious. On it are the initials of John Selcraig and Euphan Mackie, the parents of Alexander Selkirk, the man it is said who inspired Daniel Defoe to base *Robinson Crusoe* on. Born in Lower Largo in 1676, a statue of him can be seen on the village main street upon the house that sits in the location of his shoemaker father's cottage. Selkirk's character, it would seem, was far removed from Defoe's Yorkshire-born Crusoe, who displayed the more wholesome moral trails of the author. The only record connected to Selkirk in his younger years comes from the proceedings against him when he stood before the kirk session of Largo for fighting with his brothers. Heading off to sea did nothing to dampen his temper, for in 1704 after an argument with his captain he was marooned for four years and four months on the uninhabited island of Juan Fernandes with only his sea chest, which contained few bodily comforts and some books, including a Bible. He told his rescuer, Captain Rodgers, that for the first eight months he fought melancholy, spending his time building twin huts, reading his Bible and singing psalms, declaring he had never been a better Christian before or since. Captain Rodgers took Selkirk into his service as a mate and in this time gained a £800 prize. In 1714, a smart man in a naval uniform entered the kirk during a service at Largo with none but his mother recognising him. The passion for the sea called to him however, and he returned once more. He died of yellow fever in 1721 while a lieutenant of the *Weymouth* and was buried at sea, leaving behind a common-law dairymaid wife from Fife and a church-married barmaid wife from Devon. As there is no memorial for him, his parents' age-weathered memorial has attracted visitors who bring shells.

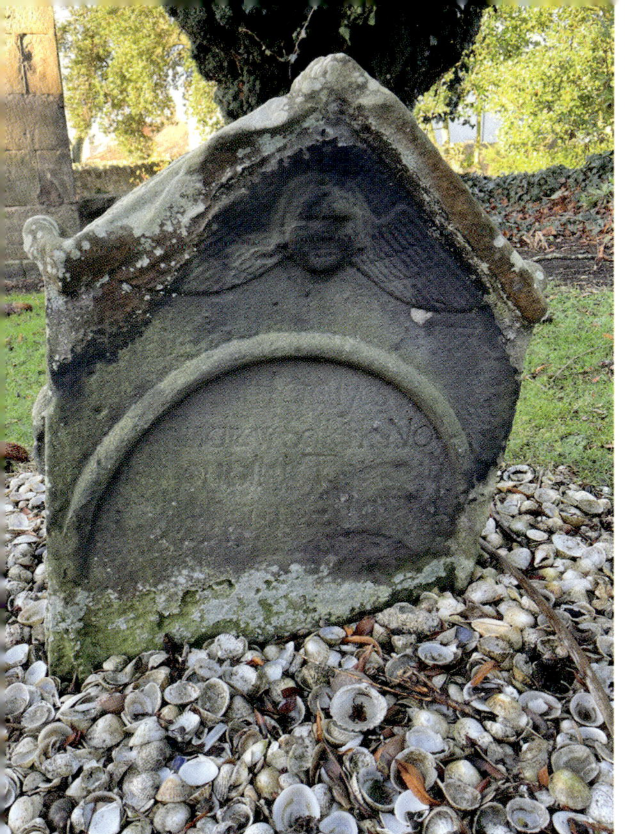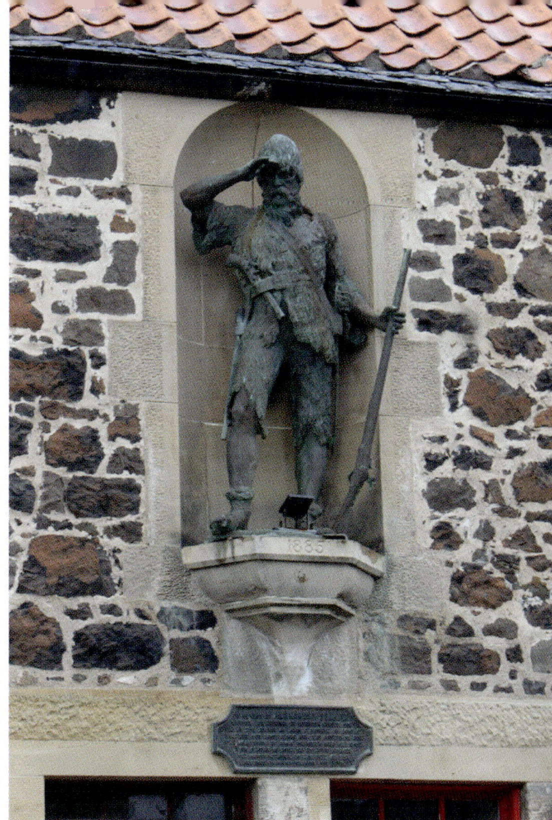

Above left: Grave of Alexander Selkirk's parents.

Above right: Statue of Alexander Selkirk.

The Largo Stone, or to call it by its former name, the Largo Cross, can be found under a shelter to the right when entering the kirkyard at the top of the stairs. Discovery is credited to General James Durham in 1839 on the family estate at Largo in two separate locations. The first is employed as a drain cover, while the other is about half a mile away at Norrie's Law. The general had the two halves reunited and erected in the grounds of Largo House. After his death his widow moved to Polton House, east of Edinburgh, and had the stone erected in her garden. It was eventually returned to Largo and placed within its protective cage – no doubt to deter any more ideas of garden landscaping. It dates from around the eighth century when wealthy Pictish families went to great lengths to display their Christian faith alongside that of their ancestors. The huge ringed cross is 6 feet in height and is still clear to see, though its Celtic knotwork and accompanying carvings have not weathered so well. A description by John Stuart in 1857 states that to the right of the cross are two intertwined creatures, likely kelpies, while to the rear three huntsmen on horseback are hunting with a pair of hounds. A double disc and Z rod accompany a mysterious 'Pictish beast' and two deer fleeing the hounds. While it is a shame that we can no longer see these carvings, it is further evidence of the importance of documenting our heritage for future generations.

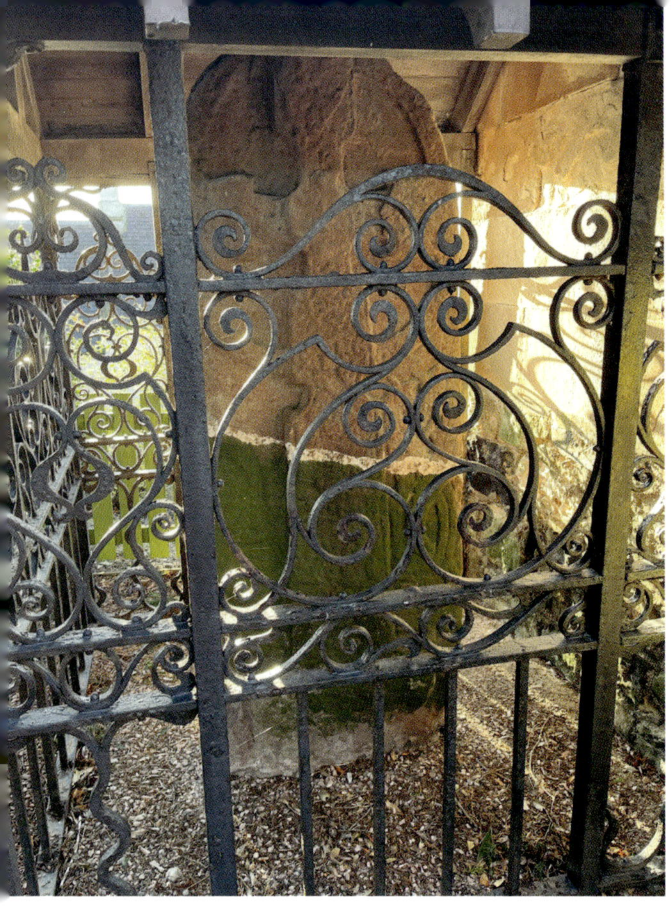

Largo Pictish stone.

Pittenweem

Due to the proximity of most of the East Neuk burial grounds being so close to the sea they are especially eroded, something that is evident in the stones at St Monans. The most poignant memorial to be found in Pittenweem is not in the churchyard of St John's, but stands down at Mid Shore, the watery graveyard of the men and women who made their living from the sea yet died and were lost in its dark depths. The memorial is that of a woman dressed in the traditional garb of fish wives of East Neuk. Her gaze is haunted as she scans the horizon for the sign of a returning boat that will never come back, the child beside her looking up as her absent-minded hand rests reassuringly on their head. It has been estimated that around 400 lives have been lost in the East Neuk stretch of the Firth of Forth since the early nineteenth century, with the majority of the families never having a body recovered to be buried on land. It may be surprising to discover that this beautifully sad memorial was only installed in September 2019 after a relentless and successful fundraising drive by the Pittenweem Fishermen's Memorial Association. The £75,000 life-sized bronze statue was created by Scottish artist Alan Herriot, with inspiration drawn from renowned painter John McGhie (1867–1952) who favoured Pittenweem and took much inspiration from the women who worked in and around the harbour.

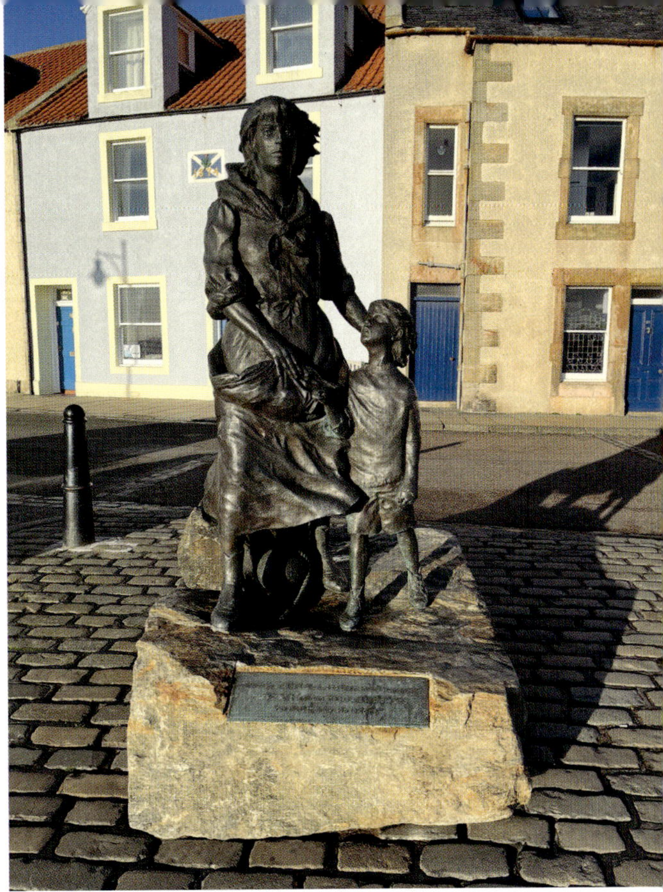

Pittenweem fishermen's memorial.

Anstruther

Driving between the Wester and Easter Anstruther over the Dreel Burn you pass 'The Buckie Hoose', the decorative creation of slater Alexander 'Sandy' Batchelor. Born in Anstruther in 1795 to parents Ninnian Bachelor and Lindsay Burn, he had a lifelong love of the sea, which would lead him to be considered a local eccentric. He was often seen on hands and knees scouring the beaches from Fife Ness to Largo looking for the little John O'Groats shells known as buckies. He used these to decorate his home both outside and in, making a little shell grotto that he turned into a museum. Among his curiosities was his star attraction – his shell-covered coffin. On his doorstep stood a sign:

> Here is the famous grotto room
> The likes not seen in any toon
> Those that do it wish to see
> Its only three pence asked as fee

For an extra penny Sandy would oblige visitors by crawling into his coffin. When he died on 13 April 1866 it was reported in the *Evening Courant* a week later that he was indeed buried in his shell-covered coffin as per his wishes.

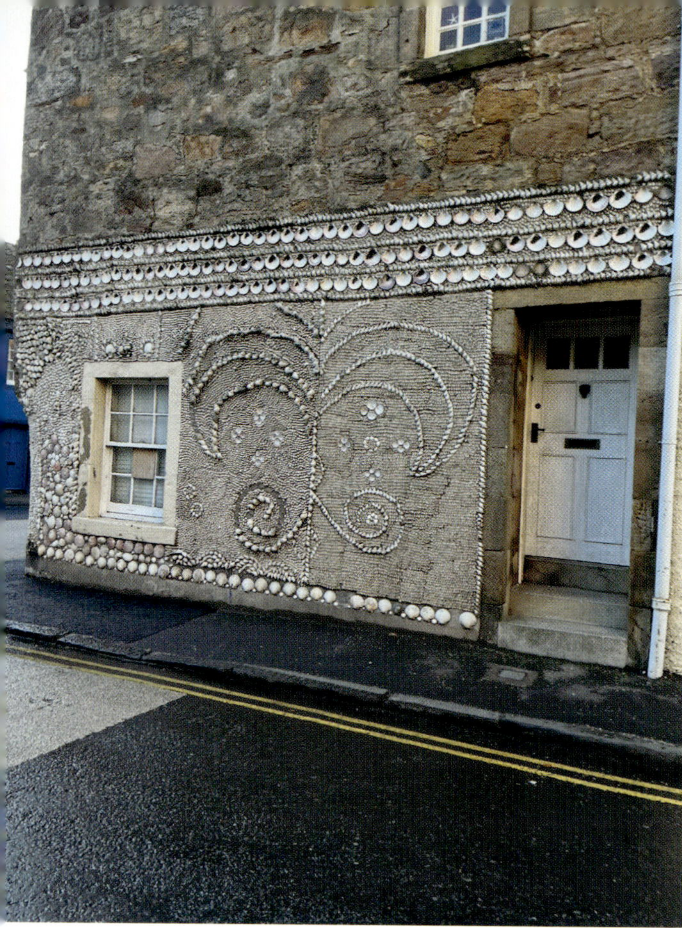

Left: The 'Buckie Hoose'.

Below: Anstruther Wester.

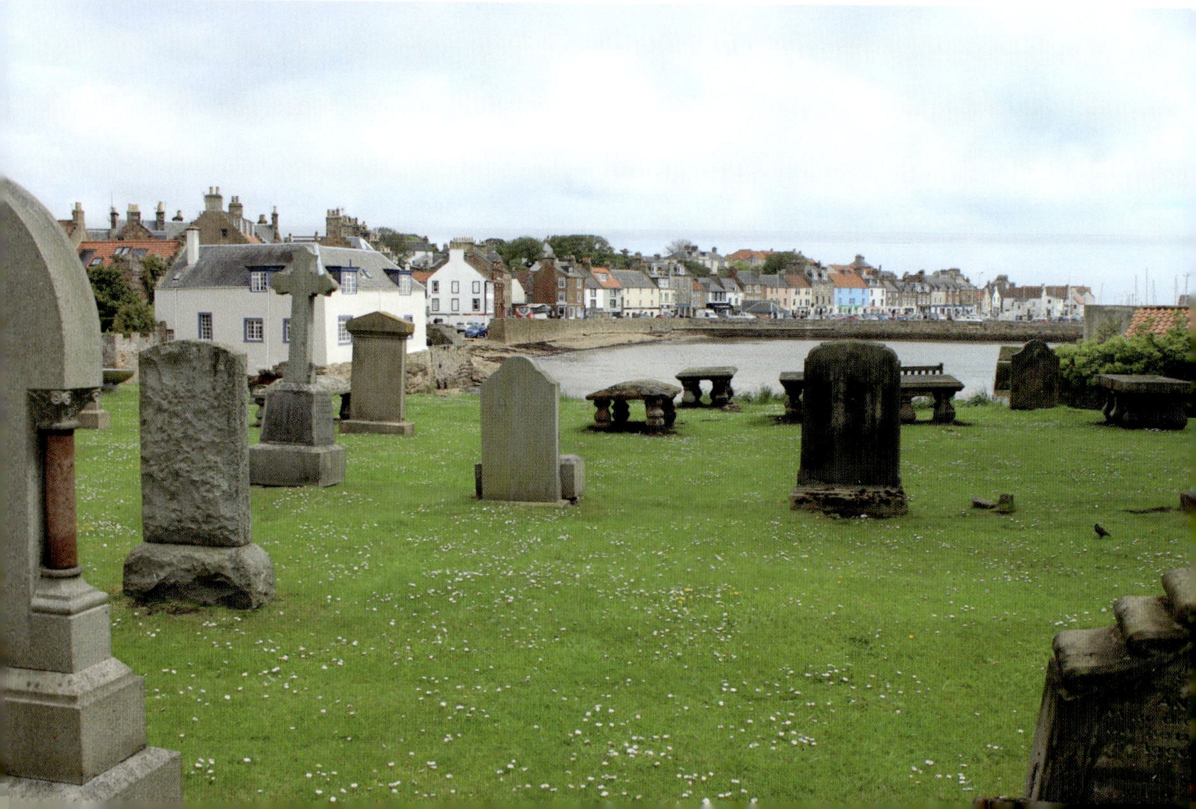

Crail

Crail Parish Church, No. 5 Marketgate, KY10 3TH
Records show that the original building dates from 1175 and for a time belonged to the Cistercian nuns of Haddington. During the Reformation the church was left intact, and John Knox came to preach his own brand of fire and brimstone in June 1559. The most notable minister, however, was James Sharp, who would later become Archbishop Sharp. There is an interesting tale concerning the church and one of its stones, though not a gravestone. In the 1100s the Devil, intent on causing mischief, disguised himself as a mason and approached the master mason in charge of building a new church at Crail. Bartering his way into a job with boasts that he would have the building constructed in no time at all, he was taken on. Indeed, the structure seemed to quickly take shape, with the new mason able to work much faster than his counterparts. But the building was growing a little too quickly, making people of Crail suspicious that the hand of the Devil was involved. Attention turned to the new mason who, furious at being discovered, dropped his disguise and flew to the Isle of May several miles offshore. His temper reaching searing heights, he seized a boulder, melting a thumb mark into its surface, and flung it at the church. The boulder split in two, with one half falling on the beach at Balcomie and the other (with the thumbprint) falling short of the building in Crail.

The Blue Stane thrown by the Devil.

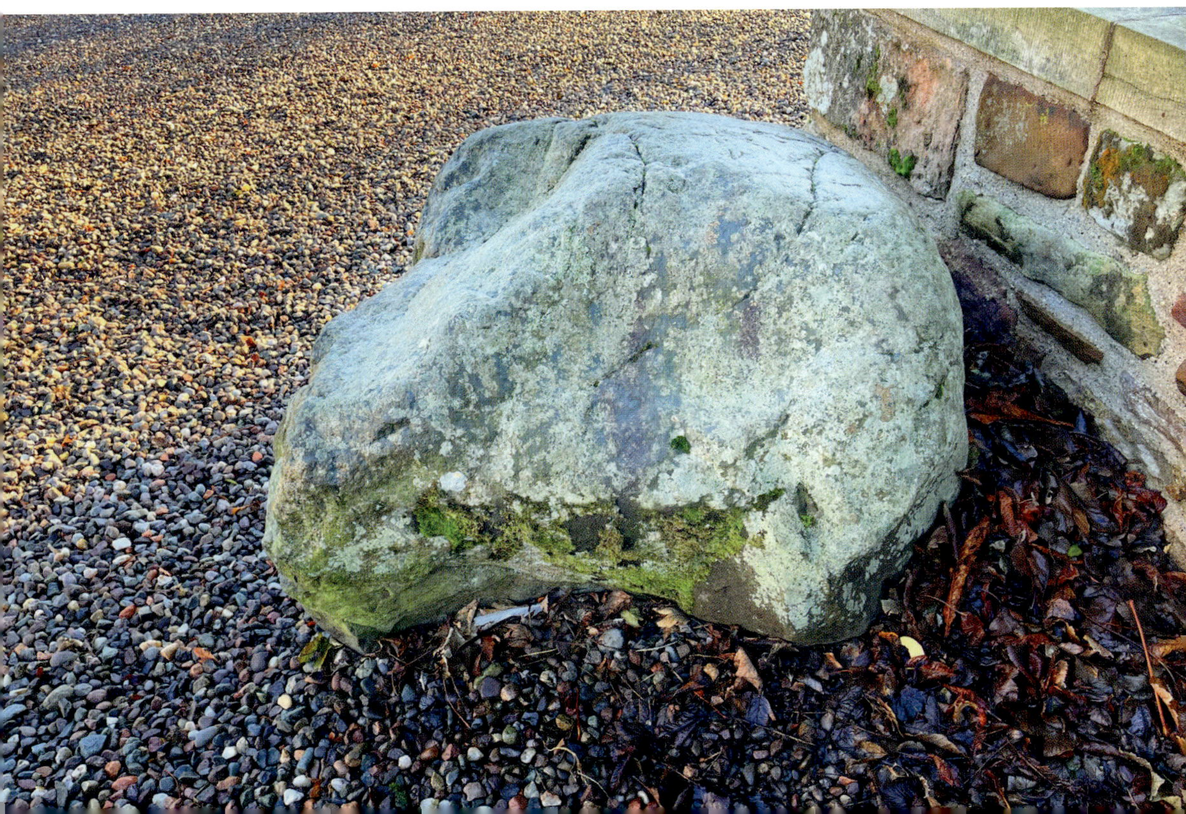

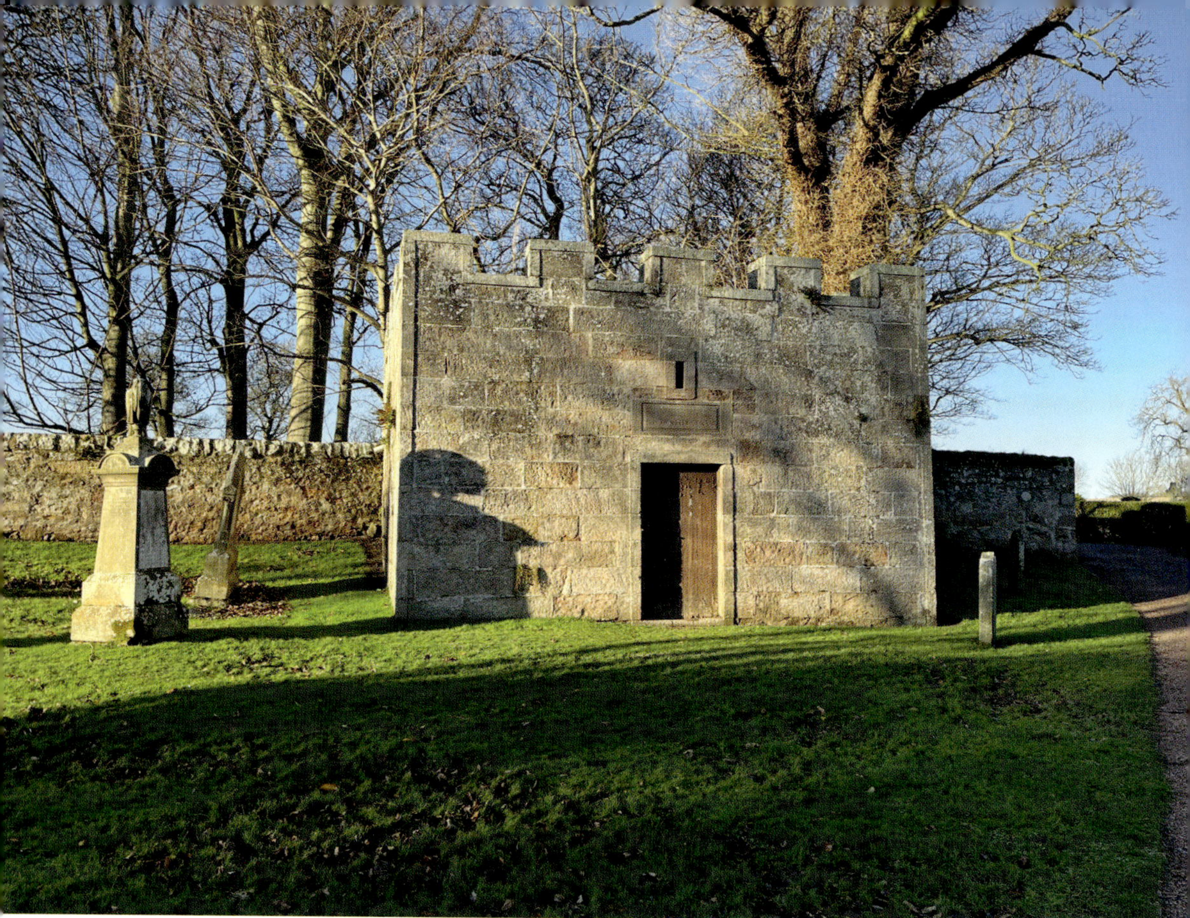

Crail Mort House.

To the rear of the church is what can only be described as Scotland's grandest and most regal-looking mort house. Built in 1824, this solid fortress for the dead complete with castle-like crenelations around the top presented no doubt as to its purpose, with the carving above the door stating: 'Erected for securing the dead. Ann dom MDCCCXXVI'.

St Andrews

Blackfriars Chapel Ruin, South Street, St Andrews, KY16 9QW
All that remains of the Blackfriars in St Andrews is the circa 1525 three-sided north transept of the chapel. This fragment of the building is the only example of its type in Scotland. There has been much debate as to whether Cardinal David Beaton was laid to rest there; however, it has generally been accepted by most that he was buried in the chapel of Blackfriars in 1547, as averred by Sir James Balfour. He was one of those involved in the murder of the cardinal and was subsequently detained on a French galley ship. The murder of the cardinal happened on 28 May 1546 when a group of Fife Protestant lords, led by Norman Leslie, Master

of Rothes, managed to enter St Andrews Castle and gain access to the cardinal's room, with threats of smoking him out if he did not open the door. The cardinal pleaded with the men, stating that as he was a prince of God they could not harm him. They could though, and they did, stabbing him a number of times. They hung his naked body out the window as evidence to the gathering people that the cardinal was dead. His body was then taken down and kept in a kist of salt in the bottle dungeon. It was later taken away in secrecy and buried.

The reason for the murder had been to wreak vengeance on Beaton, whom they declared was corrupt both morally and monetarily. As Chancellor of Scotland, Beaton enforced harsh penalties for heresy, which made him increasingly unpopular. The final straw came with the execution of George Wishart. Wishart, a Protestant reformer, would travel the country preaching against the corruption of the Catholic Church, his manner and deliverance was such that many were accepting of his word, making himself a target for Beaton's fury. He was captured and taken to St Andrews where he was tried and inevitably found guilty. The following day he was burnt at the stake on the green in front of the castle with the cardinal watching on from the window of his chambers on 1 March 1546 – the very window he himself would be hung from less than three months later.

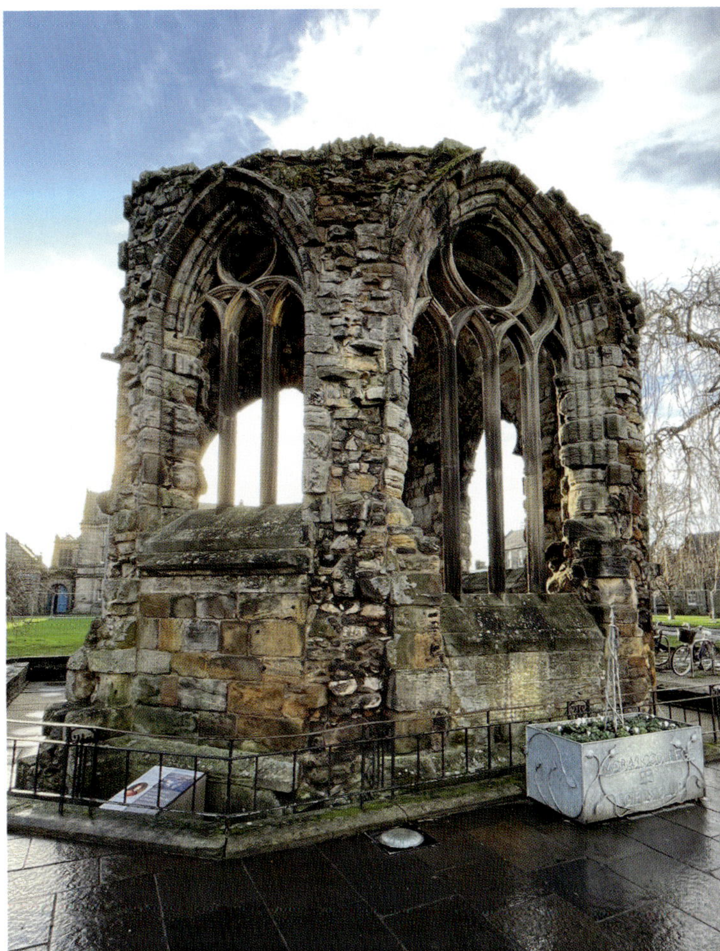

Blackfriars, South Street.

St Andrews Cathedral Graveyard and Eastern Cemetery, The Pends, KY16 9QL
While the cathedral ruins bear very little resemblance to Scotland's one-time largest religious building and the heart of the Scottish medieval Catholic Church, there is no denying that they are an exquisite location for a burial ground. In the shadow of the nearly 900-year-old St Rules Tower are the remains of the east gable of the presbytery, where the relics of Saint Andrew were once housed. It was also the final destination of pilgrims, who would walk hundreds of miles just to be nearby. It is home to stone coffins of the early bishops, and even after the Reformation many Presbyterian ministers also chose it for their final rest.

There are three more 'modern' grave sites where a sort of pilgrimage is still carried out. Golfers who travel here from all over the world are especially eager visit the grave of Allan Robertson, considered to be the first professional of the sport. The memorial is to 'Old Daw' Anderson, caddie, greenkeeper and seller of refreshments such as ginger beer from a cart near the 4th hole (now named Ginger Beer in his memory) and his son Jamie Anderson, winner of the Open Championship three consecutive years from 1877 to 1879.

It is home to the Morris family graves of Tommy Morris, golf's youngest prodigy, winning four consecutive titles in the Open Championship and his father

St Andrews Cathedral.

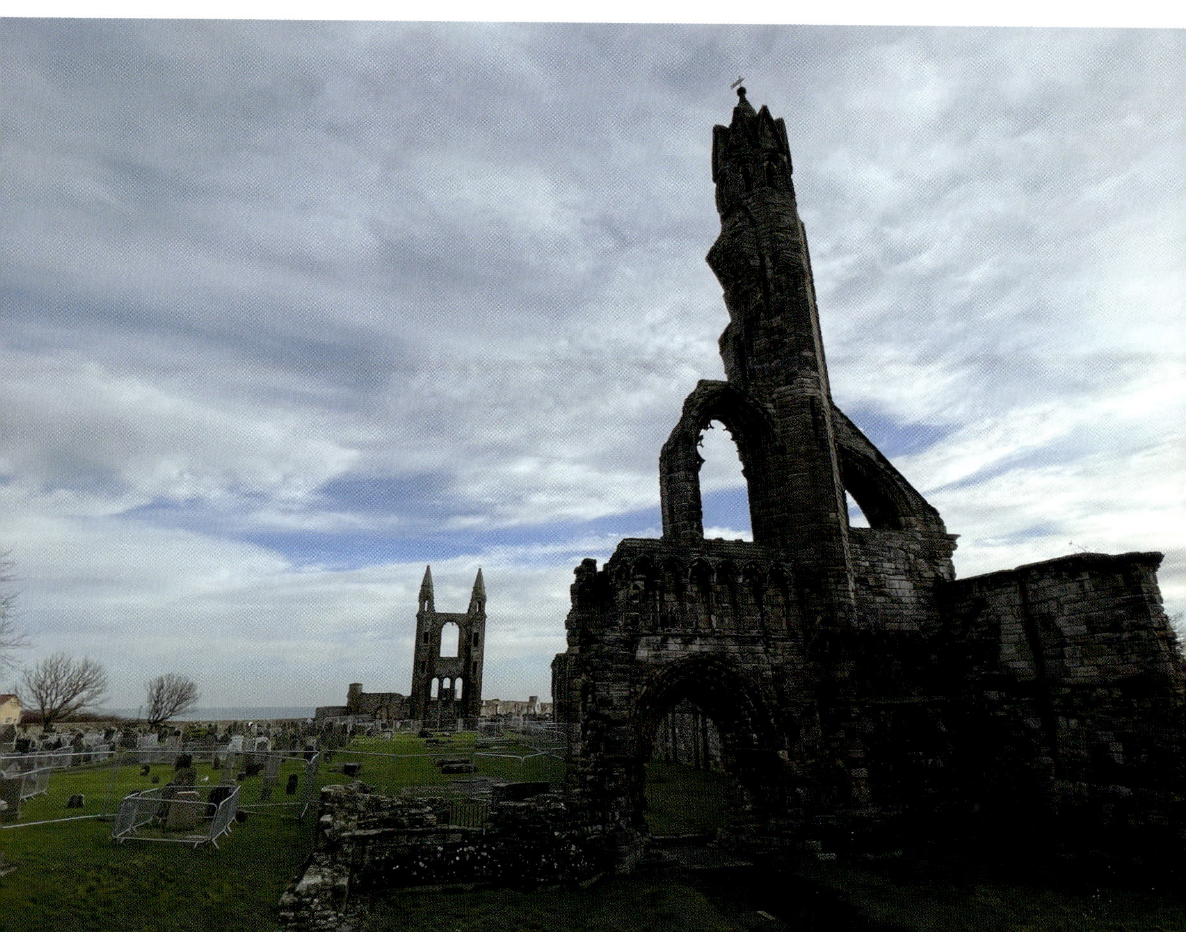

Old Tom Morris, 'the Grand Old Man of Golf'. Young Tom died at the age of twenty-four, not long after the death of his wife and son; it was said by many he died of a broken heart. Old Tom would go on to outlive his wife, his remaining sons and four grandchildren, so it is little wonder that he would continue to work right up to his own death, which was just short of his eighty-seventh birthday. Amid all the heartache he suffered, he assisted with, or solo designed, seventy-five golf courses throughout Scotland, England, Ireland, the Isle of Man and Wales. He is also considered to be 'the Father of Modern Greenkeeping'. For many decades it has been considered good luck by many golfers to leave a golf ball at the Morris grave in tribute to the great men of golf before playing on St Andrews Old Course.

The Eastern Cemetery, the 'new' section for burial, was opened in 1823 with its first funeral. There is, however, a curious little structure that looks like it has come straight from Tolkien's *The Hobbit*. The attractive yet rustic turf-covered building, accessed by a little flight of stairs, is in fact an ancient holy well dating from the days of the Celtic Catholic Church in Scotland. The little alcove above the door would once have housed a religious statue, but there is no documentation as to who it was dedicated to. It is probable it escaped ransacking during the Reformation due to it being a well and source of freshwater.

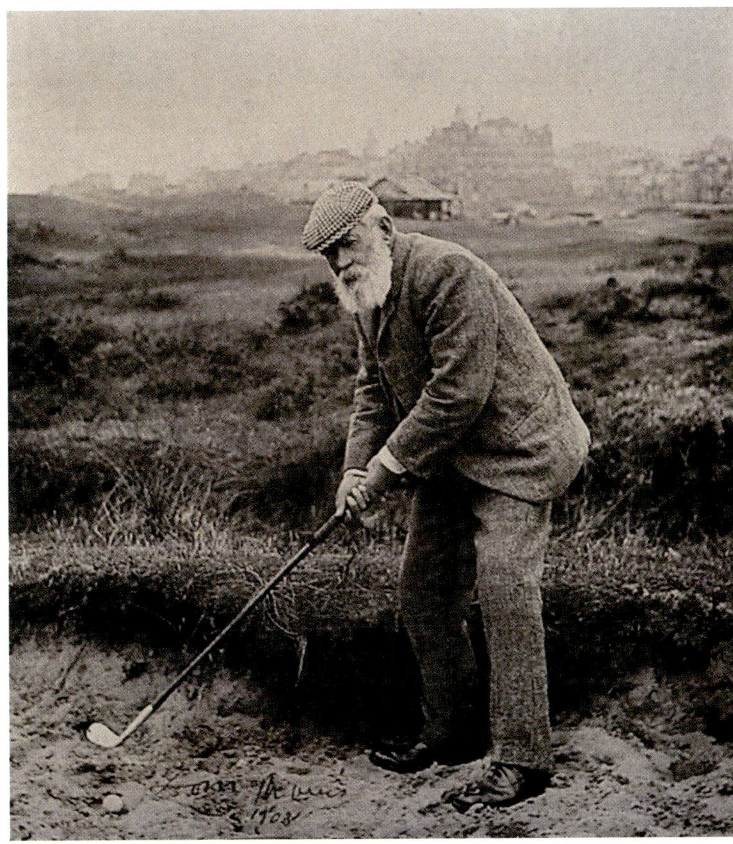

Old Tom Morris.

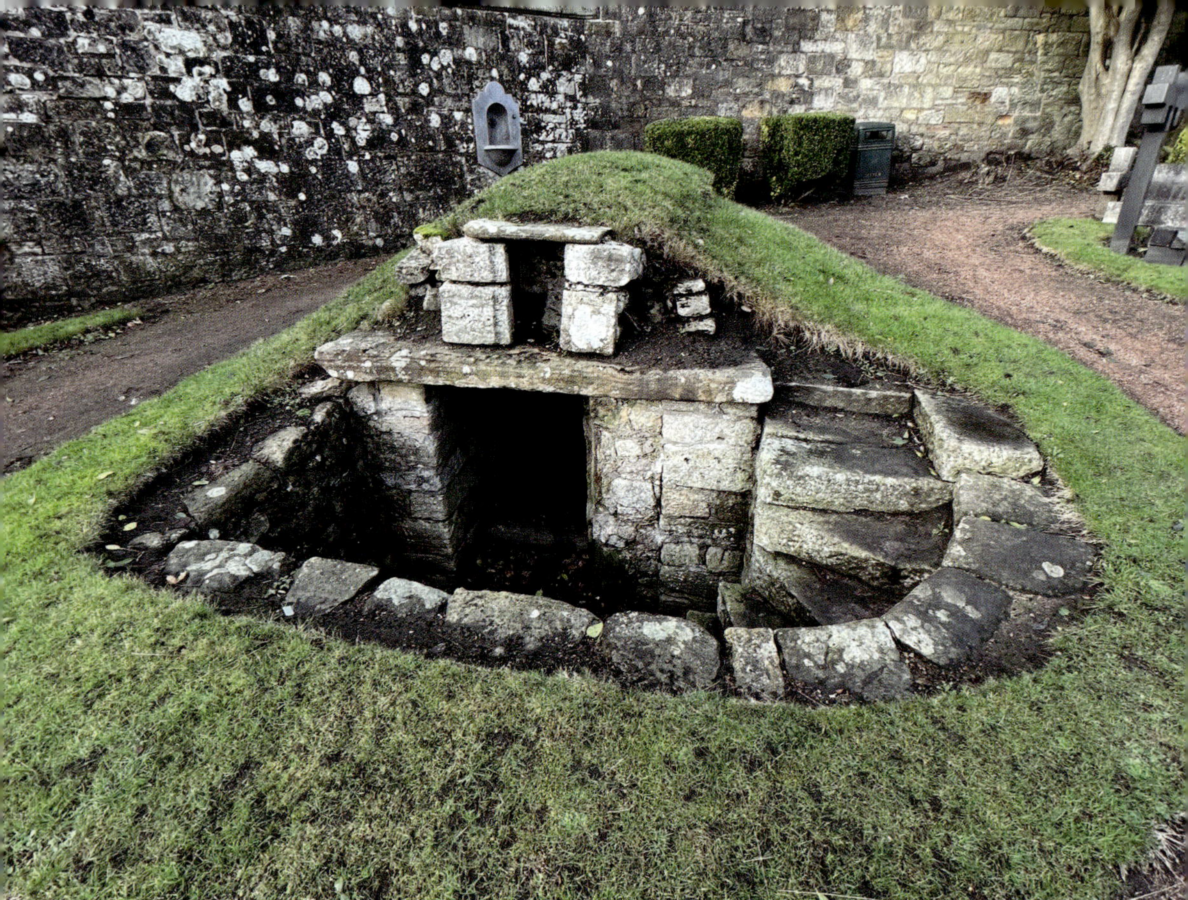

Well in the Eastern Cemetery.

Magus Muir

Bishop's Wood, By Strathkiness, KY16 9RZ

Archbishop Sharp has been mentioned several times in this book so far. He's a man who would have been well advised to remember how the people of Fife react to men of the church whom they believe act against the populace harshly, as in the case of David Beaton 133 years previously. Serving as Archbishop of St Andrews under an Episcopalian Church of Scotland from 1661 until his assassination on 3 May 1679, a day shy of his sixty-first birthday. On 2 May he was making his way from Edinburgh, lodging at Kennoway at Captain Seaton's house. The next morning he set off, stopping at Ceres to smoke a pipe with the Episcopal incumbent there. He apparently seemed unconcerned for his safety and that of his daughter as they set off in his distinctive coach over the bleak Magus Muir.

It was here that nine Covenanters had assembled with the aim of capturing or killing Sheriff Carmichael, a former baillie of Edinburgh. He was promoted to Sheriff of Fife by Sharp and ensured the severe penalties against conventicles were administered. A young lad acting as lookout informed them the archbishop's coach was approaching. The group, believing Providence had placed Sharp here, decided to change their plans and exact vengeance on him instead. David Hackston held back, proclaiming he had personal grievances with the churchman and did not want his feelings to sully the purity of their mission. While there are two conflicting accounts of what happened – one from Isabella Sharp (who witnessed her father's death) and the other from one of the covenanters – there are substantial facts that are agreed upon. Sharp was shot while in the carriage, but not killed. He was dragged from the coach so harm would not be inflicted on his daughter and, on his knees, he prayed for his life while eight of the men set upon him with swords. Hackston, true to his word, held back, neither taking part nor aiding Sharp. Isabella is said to have shouted, 'This is murder.' To which it was replied, 'Not murder, but God's vengeance on him for murdering many poor souls in the Kirk of Scotland.' The archbishop was interred at the Holy Trinity Church in St Andrews where an elaborate marble monument was erected by his son in his memory. The monument found at the spot he died is rather more rustic.

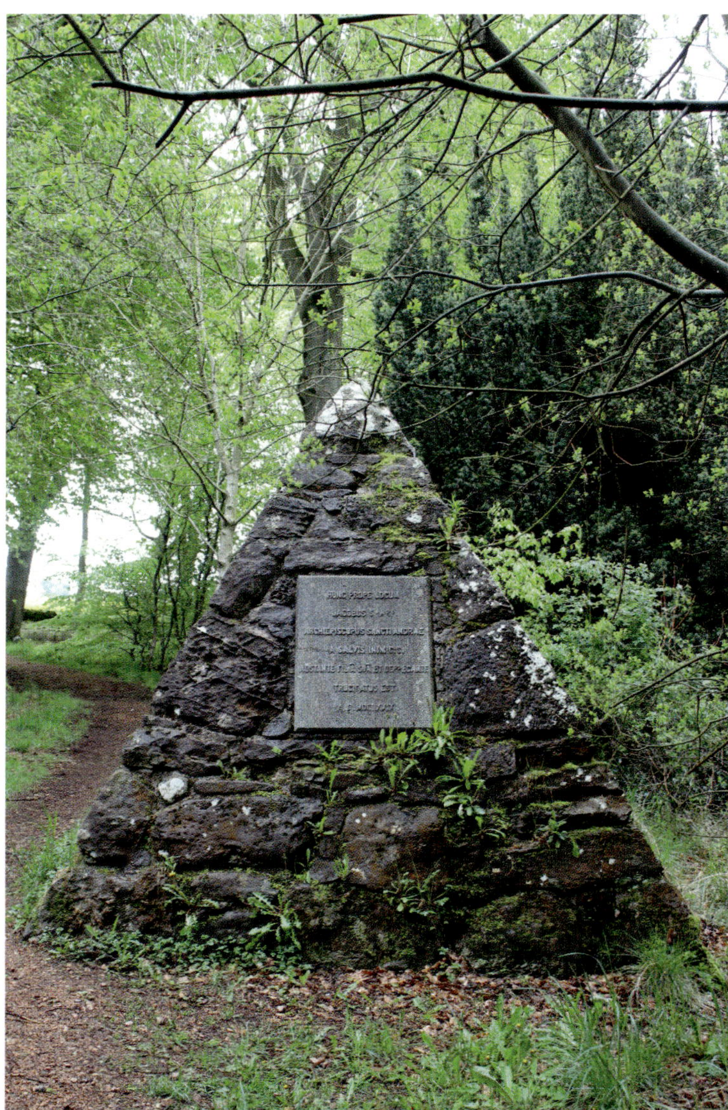

Monument to Archbishop Sharp.

Nearby is another gravestone to five Covenanters executed here as vengeance for the death of Sharp, even though they had no part in the murder. Thomas Brown, James Wood, Andrew Sword, John Weddell and John Clyde were with those captured after the Battle of Bothwell Bridge along with about 1,200 others, and were taken to Edinburgh where they were held in the exposed location of Greyfriars Kirkyard, part of which is still known today as the Covenanters' Prison. Over the next five months some succumbed to starvation or exposure while others took up the chance of liberty by signing a bond forbidding them ever taking up arms against the king. Of those left these five men were chosen and taken to Magus Muir, executed and buried here on 25 November 1679. It would actually be another four years until the second of the nine men who were involved in the archbishop's death were captured and executed. Andrew Guillen, a weaver from Balmerino, was apprehended and held at the tolbooth in Edinburgh for a month until his execution at the Mercat Cross on 13 July 1683. His body was then dispatched to Magus Muir. He was the only one of the men who physically took part in the assassination to be tried and executed.

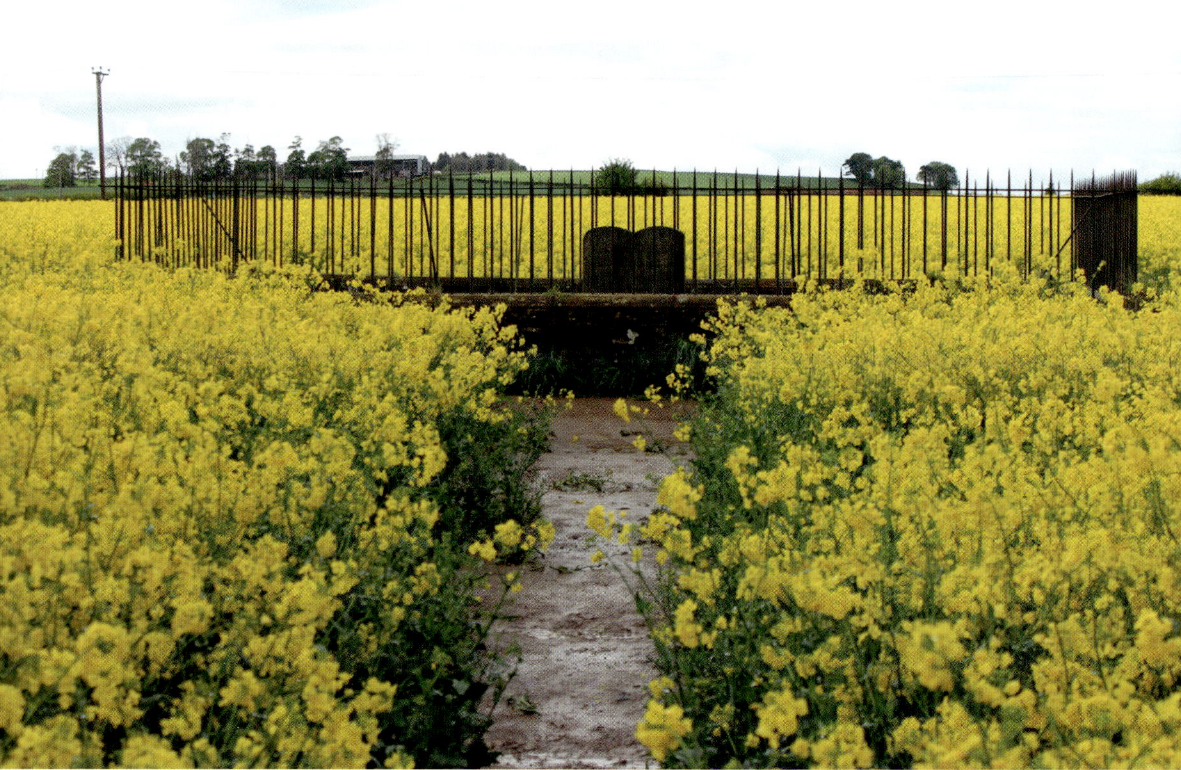

Magus Muir Martyr's grave.

Leuchars

St Athernase Church truly demands the attention of visitors. It is not only one of Scotland's oldest churches but is arguably one of the most beautiful. To the east end the Norman builders showcased their skills with the stunning chancel and apse, now over 800 years old. This part is what remains of the building that Robert de Quinci had built to honour his Norman crusader father and his mother, the daughter of a Celtic war chief. The west end is a replacement nave, having gone through some collapses and demolitions. The west tower collapsed around 1638 and the tower over the apse was replaced with the pretty 'pepper pot' seen today. In 1843, the nave was demolished and a separate church was built. The budget did not stretch to the east end (thankfully), and this was preserved rather than replaced. The champion of the church was Reginald Farlie, who in 1914 reintegrated the chancel with the nave and restored the external arcading. Of the stones, there are many to charm visitors, with varying designs. And with the unique geography on its small yet steep hill, viewing them all can be an interesting quest.

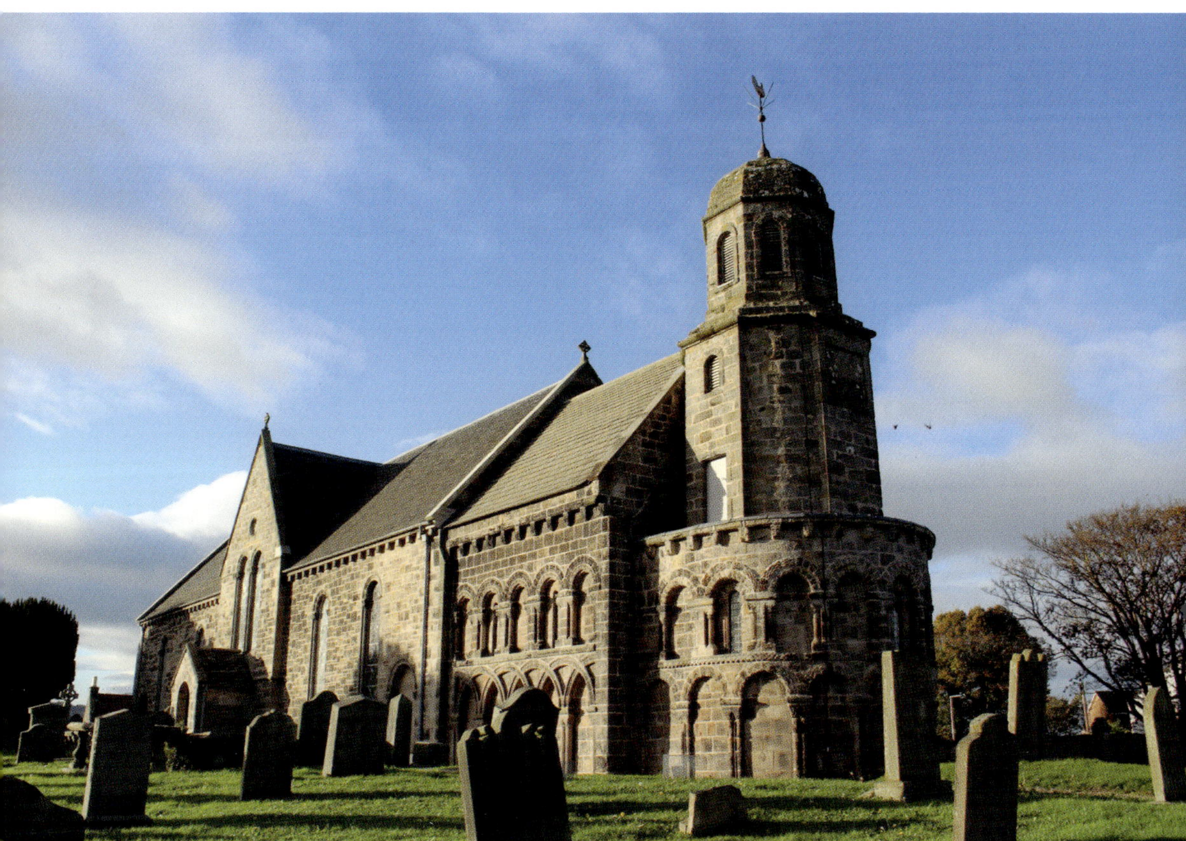

St Athernase Church.

Forgan

The parish of Forgan contains two rather spectacular burial grounds just a short distance from each other. Turning off the A914 and heading east, you come to the turn off for the newer of the two – Vicarsford Cemetery. Its impressive memorial chapel sitting high above much of the grounds, visitors would be forgiven for assuming this little piece of French Gothic reconstruction complete with gargoyles was much older than a Victorian creation. Sir John Leng commissioned local architect Thomas Martin Cappon to build the chapel in 1894 to honour his wife Emily, who had died the previous year and had been the first to be buried in the new Vicarsford Cemetery.

Taking the little grass path down the slope to the south of the chapel is a simple, lone white cross. At the foot of the cross are a number of toys – a couple of trucks, a boat and a little figurine. New artificial flowers beam out from the grass, while some of their older counterparts seem to be fading into the background. Norman Galbraith Smith was only six when he died. Born into a wealthy clothier family, his father, unable to cope with grief, became a minister and moved his family to Australia. While little Norman was left behind, it is evident after all these years he is still visited and cherished in locals' hearts.

Vicarsford Memorial Chapel detail.

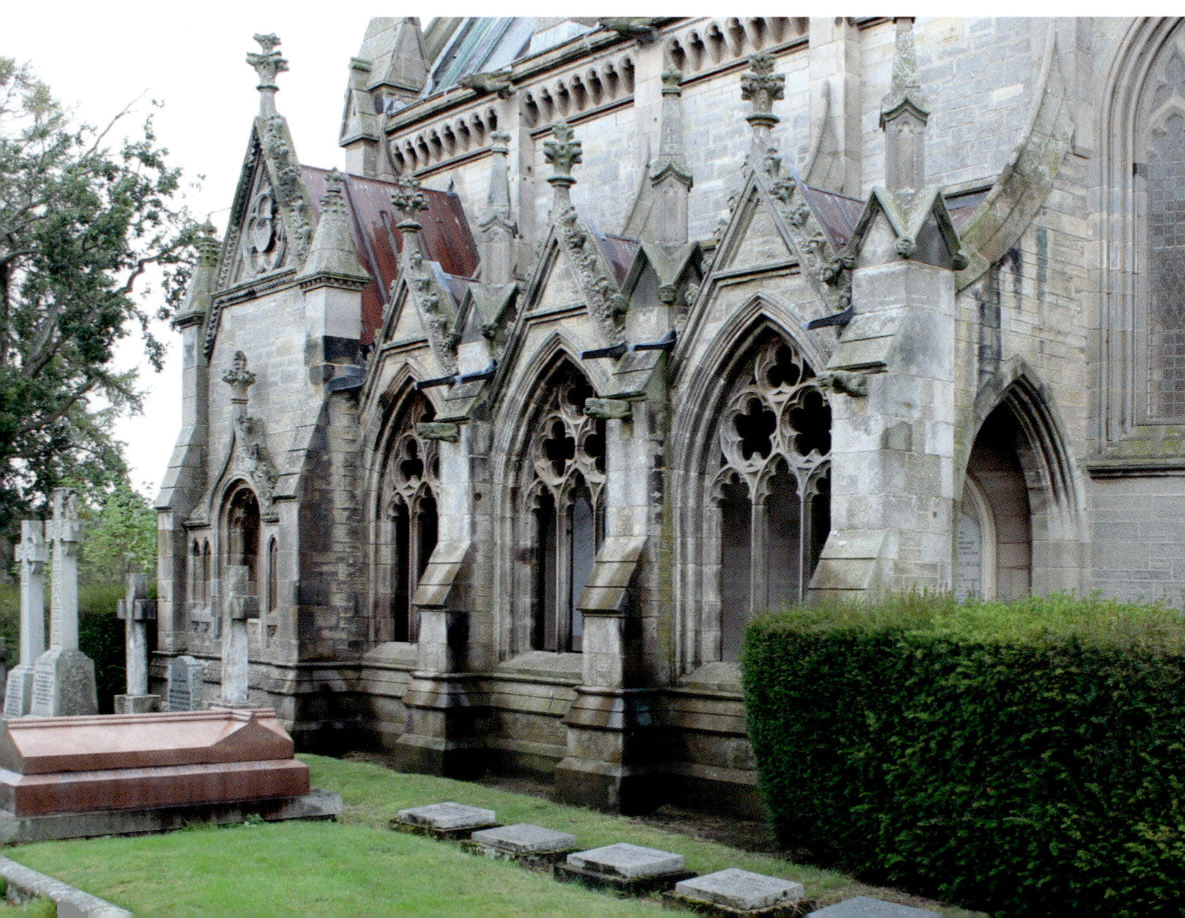

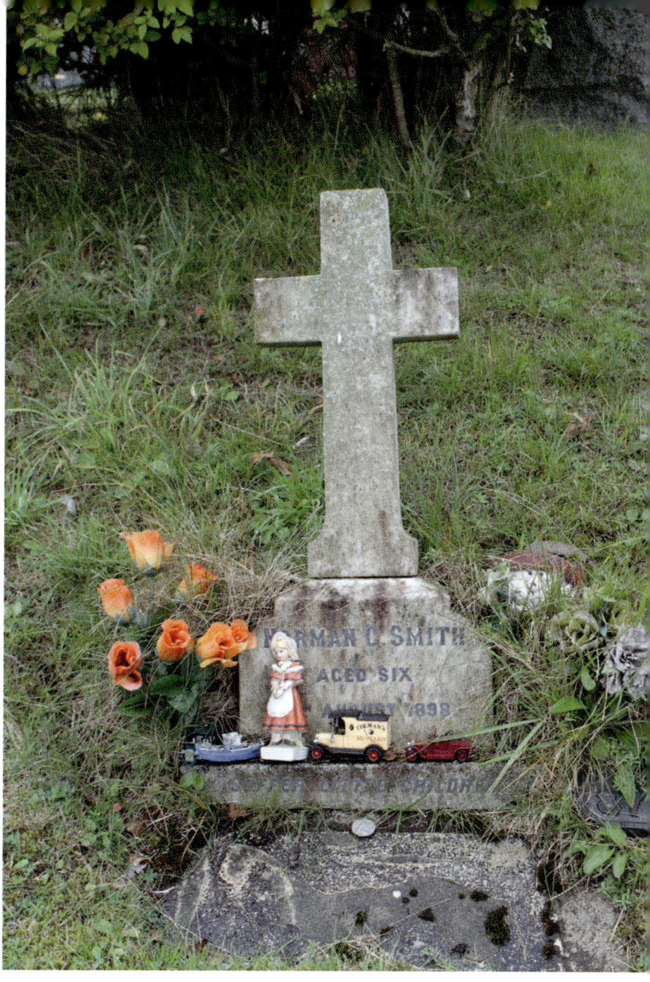

Little Norman Smith.

The *Mars* training ship was a well-known sight at Woodhaven Harbour at Wormit. Often described as a Dundee training ship, it took in both Protestant and Catholic boys, which meant children were sent from all over Britain. It was for children thought to be wayward or who might potentially be led into lives of crime; however, its very first recruit, No. 1 on the register of 1869, Murdoch McLeod, was a volunteer. A thirteen-year-old bookbinder's apprentice from Perthshire, he failed to become a stowaway on a ship bound for Russia and craved adventure on the seas. After completing his training on the *Mars* he joined the merchant navy where he served for many years before finally settling in Wellington, New South Wales (about 230 miles from the sea), and eventually became its major. While his was a success story, there were others who were not so fortunate. In a quiet corner of the cemetery is a large rock memorial, which lists the names of thirty-eight boys who died serving on the *Mars* between April 1895 and January 1928. Deaths ranged from illness to drowning, either by accident or misadventure. While the training by today's standards would be considered harsh, it's third captain was considered strict but not cruel. Captain Augustus Lennox Scott joined the *Mars* as its captain at the age of thirty-six, replacing his own father, Charles, captain for twenty-three years. Together the two Scott captains served just shy of fifty years.

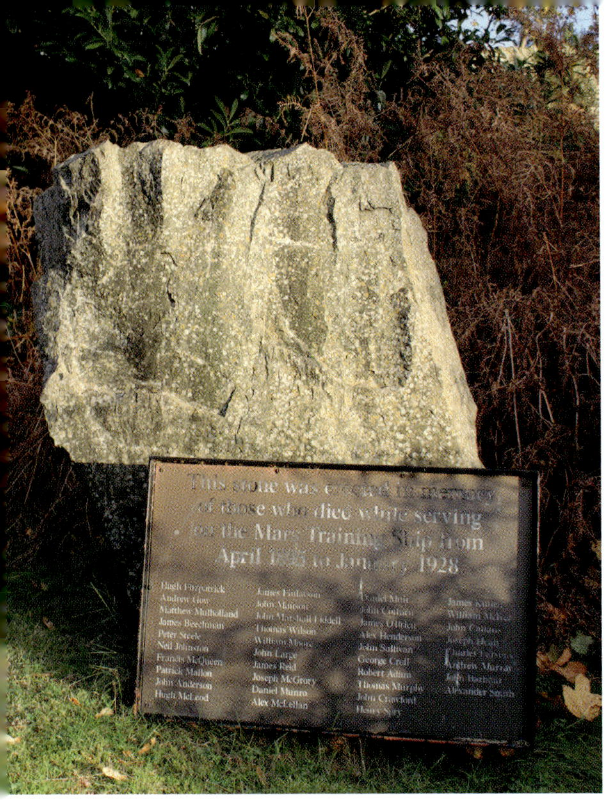 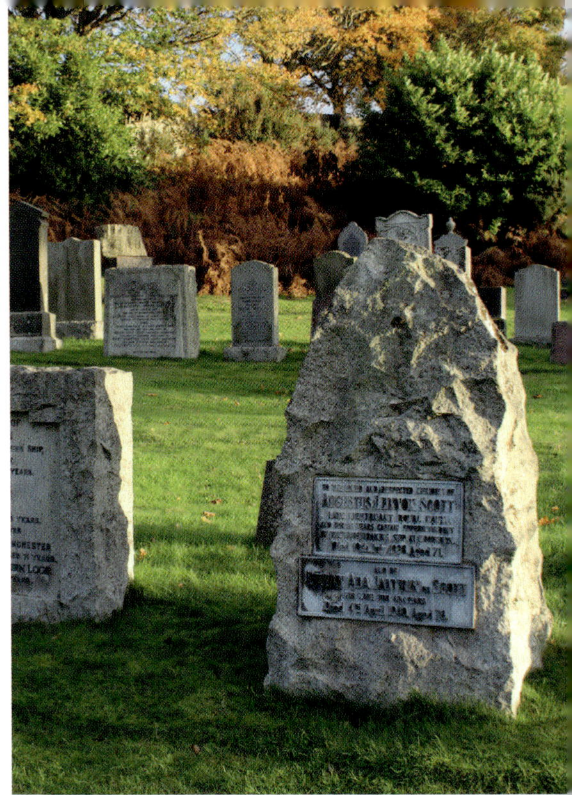

Above left: *Mars* boys' memorial.

Above right: Captain A. L. Scott of the *Mars* training ship.

Below: *Mars* training ship.

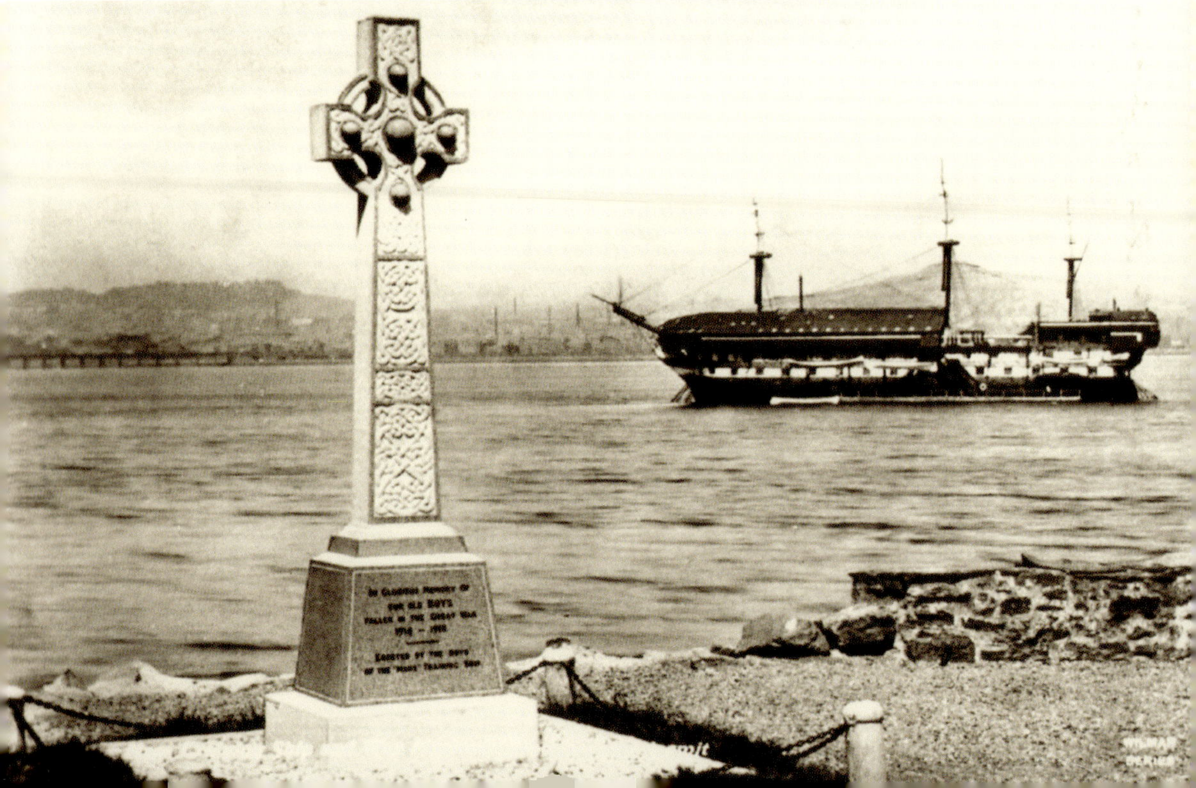

Travelling further down the road you come to St Fillan's Old Kirkyard. The ruined kirk has been recently stabilised by the Heritage Team at Fife Council, whose aim is to save these beautiful ruins from further erosion by repointing some of the old stonework and rebuilding walls with bricks that will blend into the structure. Here is one of the best gardener's stones to be found in Fife. It is carved from sandstone from the Angus region, which, although harder to carve, stands the test of time and looks quite fresh. More examples of stone from Angus can be found at Ferryport-on-Craig's graveyard.

It is also in this little burial ground where more of the *Mars* boys have been laid to rest. The very first three boys to die in 1871 have their own gravestone here: 'Who in a fit of waywardness incidental of youth left Woodhaven Pier in an open boat on the stormy morning of March 13th 1871.' A second memorial is for the *Mars* boys who died and were interred there between 1910 and 1920. There is no clear record of how many boys died on the *Mars* over seventy years as casual research produces names without the memorial dates.

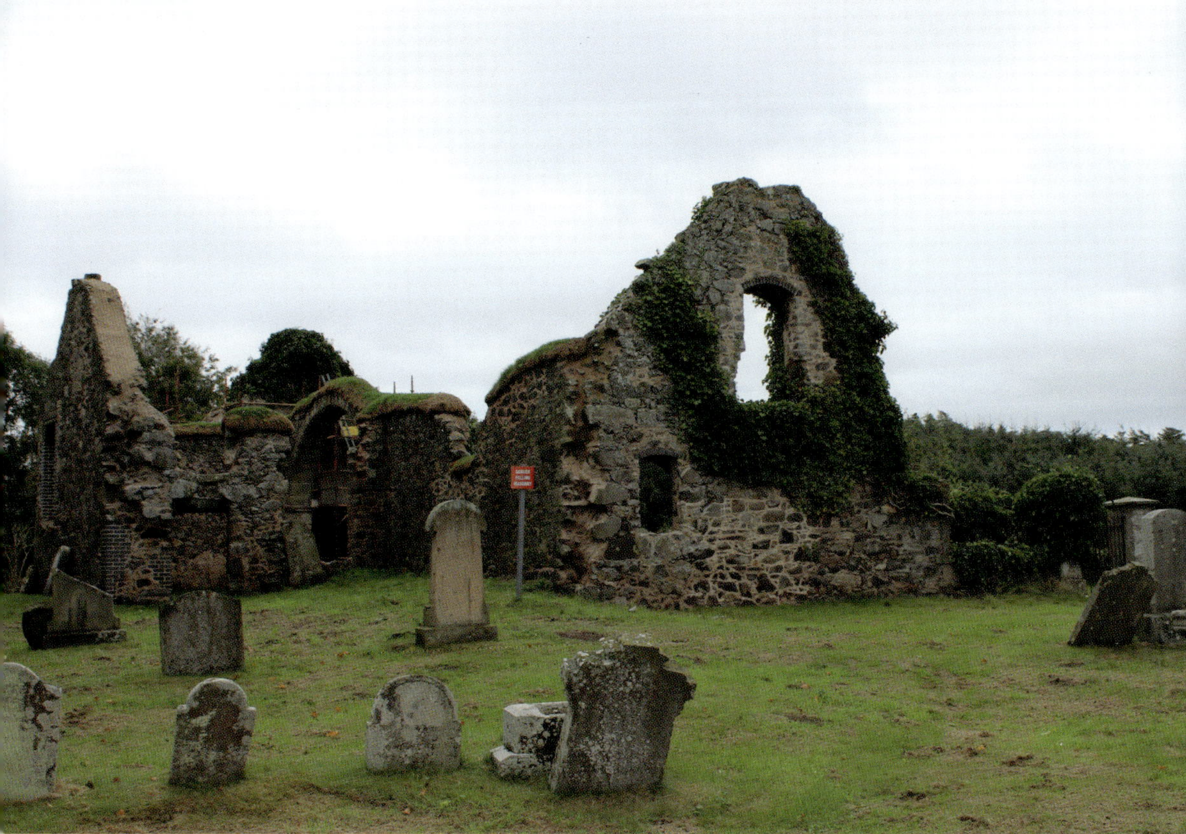

St Fillan's Old Kirk.

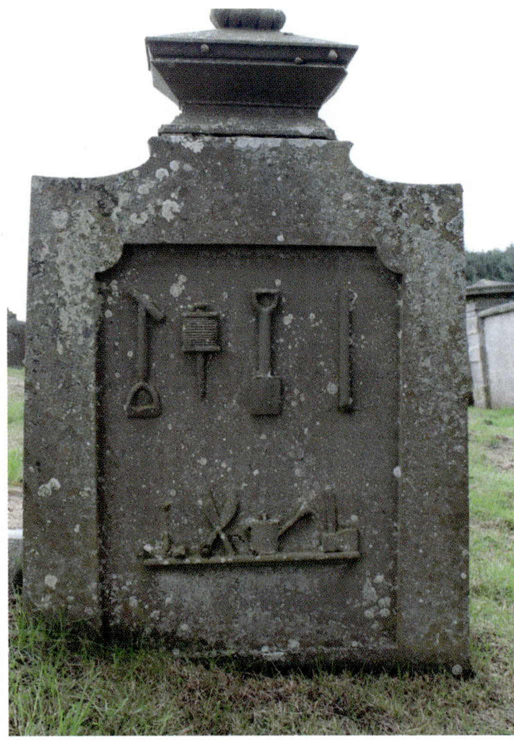

Gardener's Stone.

It is an important period of the area's history and should be remembered by some of the other notable events the boys were part of. When the Tay Rail Bridge collapsed it was boats from the *Mars* that first went out to look for survivors, and on subsequent days looking for bodies to return to their families. A few of the boys who served as children went on to have careers at sea before returning to work on the *Mars* and help train another generation of children. It was said that when the *Mars* was finally taken away to Inverkeithing to be broken down the shores were lined with grown men, nobody questioning the tears in some of their eyes.

Inchcolm Island

There is one burial ground that stands quite apart from any other in Fife – literally. Inchcolm is a beautiful island, dotted with an assortment of buildings spanning different eras. Its centrepiece is the impressive Augustine Inchcolm Abbey, known as 'the Iona of the East'. It is Scotland's most intact surviving monastic house, having escaped the attentions of the Reformation mobs.

Long before the abbey was founded the island was called 'Aemonia' or 'Emonia'. There have been differences of opinion as to the meaning of the name; some authorities believe it to translate to 'the Solitary Isle' while others claim it

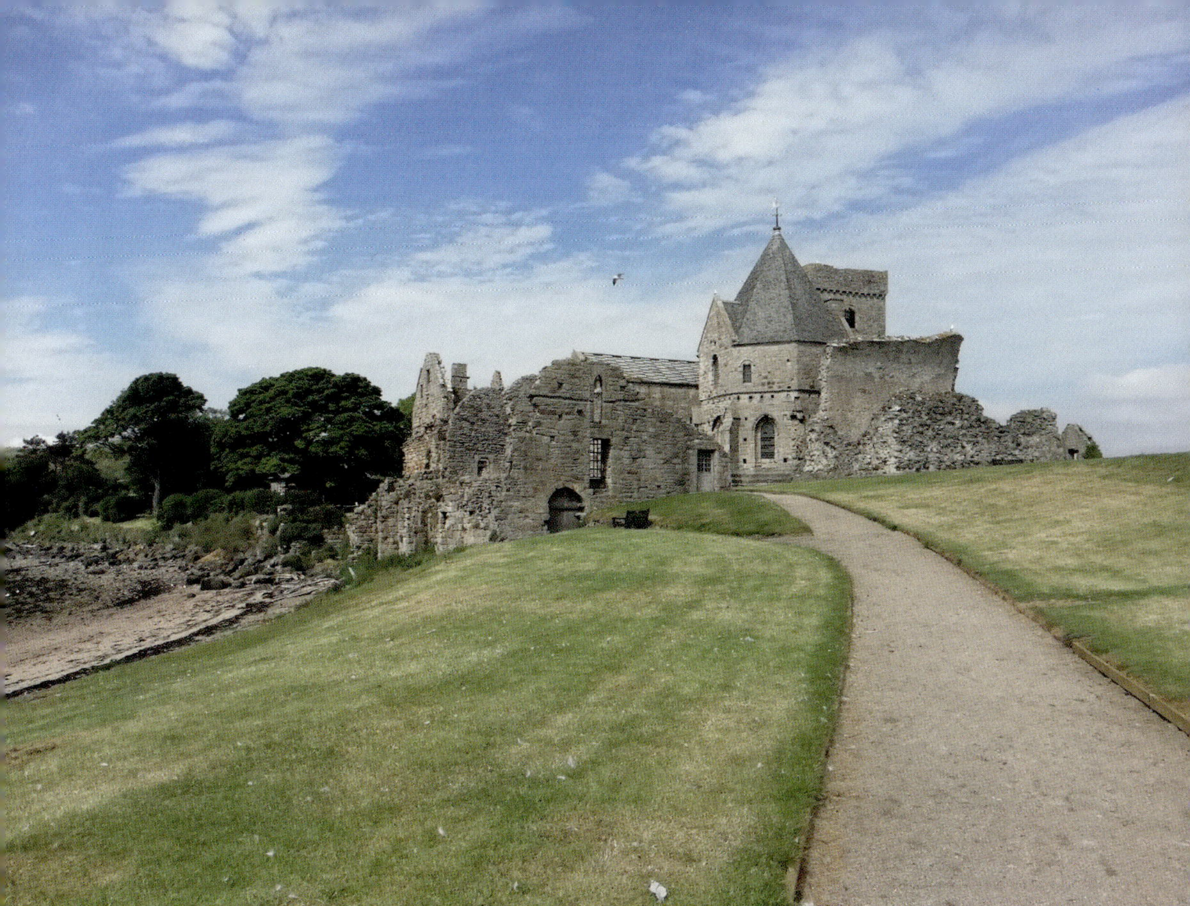

Inchcolm Abbey.

to be 'the Isle of the Druids'. As most holy sites have long traditions of being important to former religions or sacred beliefs, the latter is a worthy contender for the meaning. While Iona in the west of Scotland was considered a holy place, and as such a favoured burial place, so too was Inchcolm in the east, even by enemies in times of war who wished their fallen to rest in hallowed ground. In his *Chronicles of England, Scotland and Ireland*, Holinshed mentions that after the Battle of Kinghorn, the Danes, defeated by MacBeth, paid the king 'a great sum of gold, that such of their friends as were slain at this last bickering might be buried in Saint Colme's Inch'. William Shakespeare was known to take inspiration from Holinshed for a few of his plays, so it is little surprise that when James VI of Scotland took the English throne on Elizabeth I's death, the playwright would look to seek favour with his new Scottish king. Shakespeare described the battle as follows:

> Sweno, the Norways' king craves composition;
> Nor would we deign him burial of his men;
> Till he disbursed at Saint Colm's Inch
> Ten Thousand dollars to our general use.

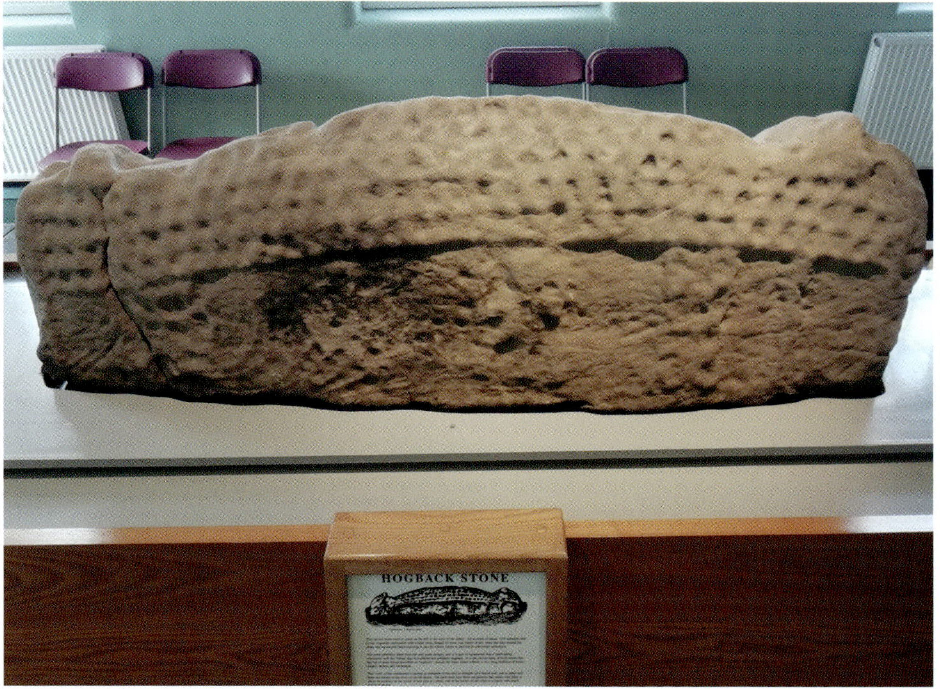

Hogback Stone.

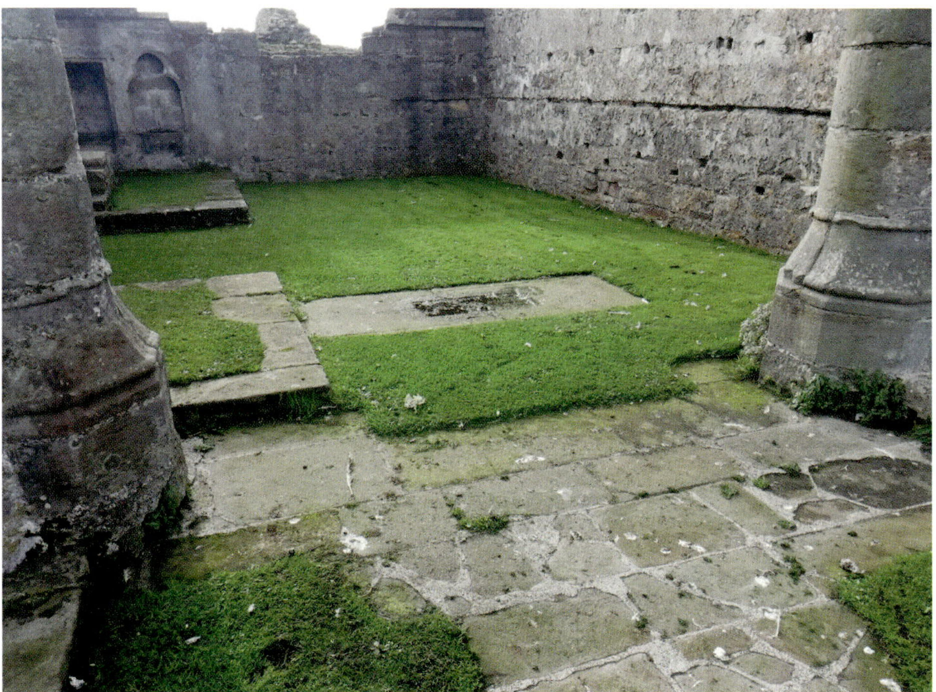

Grave slab in south transept.

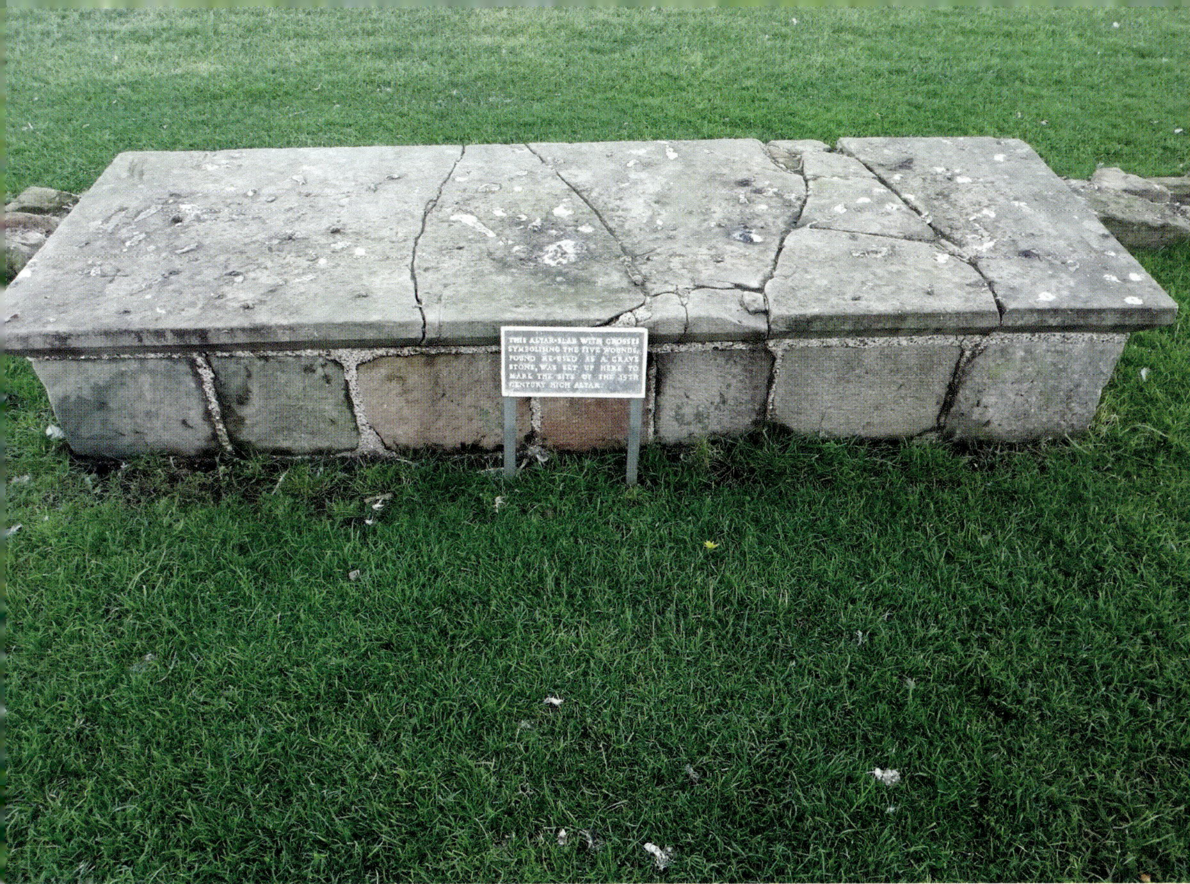

Repurposed grave slab.

While there is no firm written documentation from the period in question, there is evidence that the account is credible as a hog-backed stone dating from around the eleventh century was discovered on a grassy knoll to the west of the abbey and is now housed in the visitor centre, protected from the elements. Unfortunately, nearly a thousand years on, a lot of imagination is needed to see it how it used to look. Sir Robert Sibbald describes seeing it on a visit to the island when it was less effaced, being carved with fierce and grim faces at either end while in the middle was a figure of a man with a spear.

The year 1123 was the one that religious life on the island was to change. According to legend Alexander I and his men were forced to seek shelter during a ferocious storm that threatened to sink their vessel. The Culdee hermit who lived there provided shelter and what meagre sustenance he could from the milk of his cow and the shellfish that gathered on the shores. In thanks the king decided that a monastery would be built on the island. I can't help but feel for the hermit, who probably preferred his own company.

It is from this time that the number of burials would increase, though it should be stated that for many years the Scots had preferred to bury their dead on islands to protect them from the wild dogs that roamed the lands. There is evidence of burial within the ruins of the church building, with two flat stones still seen in the north and south transepts and the altar stone, now in its correct position, carved with five crosses, had once been reused as a grave marker.

Inchcolm, with its naturally beautiful scenery, peaceful atmosphere and a tendency to capture hearts and hold them forever, has continued to be the final resting place for some who have chosen to be cremated. The scattering of ashes in locations like this is another chapter in the history of death in Fife, leaving swathes of people defying headstones. Yet, honouring a wish is just as important and filled with as much love as commissioning the beautifully carved headstones of the past.

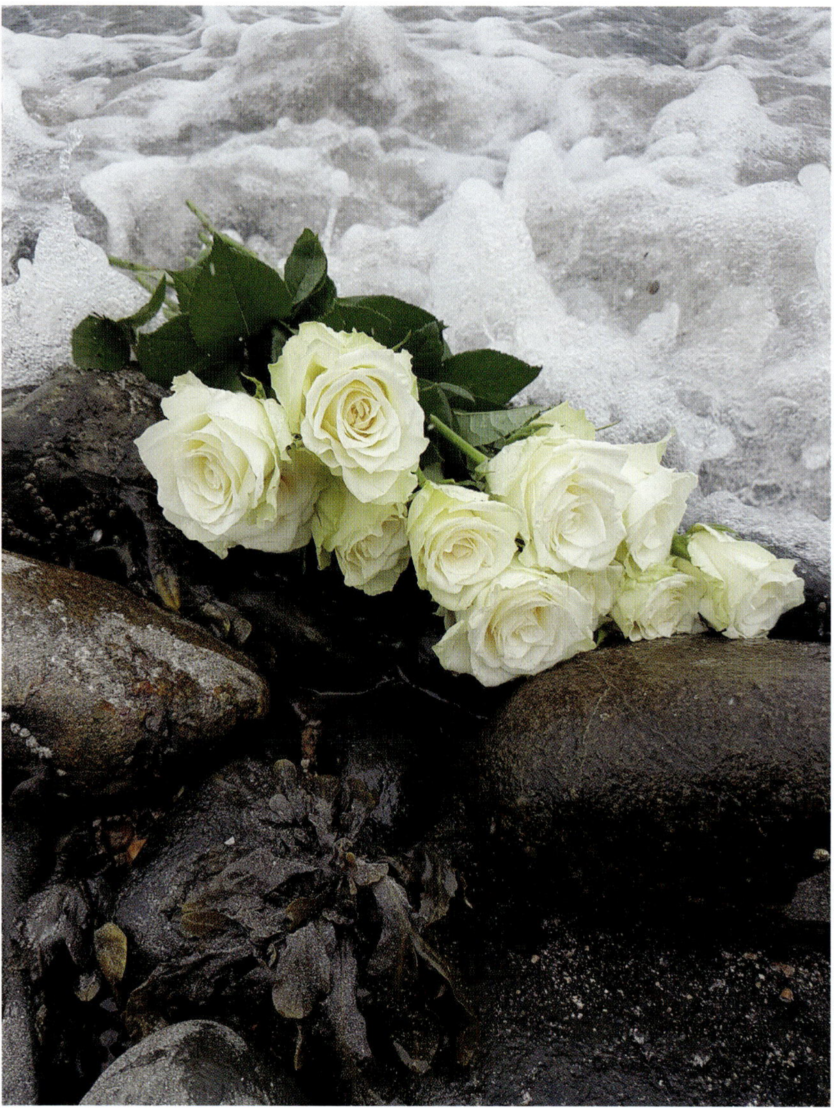

Goodbye is not forever.

8

Select Historic Burial Grounds in Fife Not Already Featured

Abercrombie Churchyard, Balcaskie Estate, KY10 2DE
Aberdour – St Fillans, Hawcraig Road, KY3 0UP
Anstruther Easter Old Kirkyard, School Green, KY10 3HF
Anstruther Wester Churchyard, High Street, Ky10 3DJ
Auchterderran, Woodend Road, Cardenden, KY5
Beath Old Church, Old Perth Road, KY4 9PS
Cairneyhill Churchyard, Main Street, KY12 8QT
Cameron Parish Church, KY16 8PD
Carnbee Churchyard, Anstruther, KY10 2RU
Carnock Old Kirkyard, Main Road, KY12 9JG
Kennoway Old Parish Graveyard, KY8 5JU
Ceres Churchyard, Kirk Brae, KY15 5NA
Creich – St Devenic's, Near Brunton
Crombie Churchyard, KY12 8LN
Dalgety Bay – Cornerstone Church, KY3 0RY
Dunbog Old Parish Church, KY14 6JF
Dunino Church, KY16 8LU
Elie Parish Church, High Street, KY9 1BZ
Ferry-Port-On-Craig, Tayport, DD6 9NS
Inverkeithing – St Peter's, Church Street, KY11 1LX
Kemback Old Parish Church, KY15 5RY
Kettle Old Churchyard, Main Street, KY15 7QR
Kilconquhar Old Parish Church, Main Street, KY9 1LQ
Kilmany Parish Church, KY15 4PT
Kilrenny Old Parish Church, Kirk Wynd, KY10 3JJ
Kinghorn Old Parish Church, Nethergate, KY3 9SY
Kinglassie Parish Church, Church Lane, KY5 0XE
Kingsbarns Parish Church, The Square, KY16 8SS
Markinch Old Church, Kirk Street, KY7 6DU
Moonzie Churchyard, School Road, KY15 4NL
Pittenweem Parish Church, Kirkgate, KY10 2LF
Saline Old Kirk, Bridge Street, KY12 9TS

Scoonie Old Kirkyard, KY8 4SZ
St Monan's Chapel, Braehead, KY10 2AL
Strathmiglo Graveyard and Pictish Stone, Kirk Wynd, KY14 7QD
St Adrian's Parish Church, West Wemyss, KY1 4SP
St Mary's by the Sea, No. 14 High Street, East Wemyss, KY1 4RU

Bibliography

Adams, Norman, *Scottish Bodysnatchers* (Goblinshead: Edinburgh, 2002)

Campbell, James, *Balmerino and Its Abbey* (Blackwood: Edinburgh, 1899)

Douglas, Gordon, *We'll Send Ye Tae the Mars* (Black and White Publishing: Edinburgh, 2008)

Findo, Martin, *Bodysnatchers* (George Weidenfeld & Nicolson Ltd: London, 1988)

Gifford, John et al, *The Buildings of Scotland: Fife* (Penguin: Middlesex, 1984)

Gordon, Ann, *Death Is for the Living* (Paul Harris Publishing: Edinburgh, 1984)

Jalland, Pat, *Death in the Victorian Family* (Oxford University Press: Oxford, 1996)

Laqueur, Thomas, *The Work of The Dead* (Princeton University Press: Oxford, 2015)

Lyle, David, *Shadows of St Andrews Past* (John Donald Publishers Ltd: Glasgow, 1989)

MacDonald, Smith, *The Witches of Fife* (Birlinn Ltd: London, 2014)

MacDougall, Ian, *Voices from Work and Home* (Mercat Press: Edinburgh, 2000)

Mackay, A. E., *A History of Fife and Kinross* (Wm Blackwood and Sons: Edinburgh, 1896)

McGill, Linda, *The Mars Training Ship* (Stevenson Ltd: Dundee, 1996)

Miller, James, *Salt in the Blood* (Canongate Books: Edinburgh, 1999)

Plant, Marjorie, *The Domestic Life of Scotland in the Eighteenth Century* (Edinburgh University Press: Edinburgh, 1952)

Proctor, Stephen, *Monarch of the Green* (Birlinn Ltd: Edinburgh, 2021)

Robertson, J. K., *About St Andrews and About* (Innes Ltd: Cupar, 1973)

Ross, Peter, *A Tomb With a View* (Headline Publishing: London, 2020)

Ross, W., *Aberdour and Inchcolme* (T&A Constable: Edinburgh, 1885)

Wills, Simon, *How Our Ancestors Died* (Pen and Sword Books Ltd: Barnsley, 2020)

Wilsher, Betty, *Understanding Scottish Graveyards* (Cronwell Press: Trowbridge, 1995)

Acknowledgements

My most heartfelt thanks go to my husband, Jamie, who has not only been supportive of my graveyard obsession but who has also been there right beside me through the last couple of years in a world that has been turned upside down and inside out. Thanks and love also goes to my son, Brandon. The list of people I would like to give my appreciation to could probably fill this whole book! The fantastic team at Amberley Publishing, my friends at HES, Kirkcaldy Old Kirk Heritage Group, FoGK, Fife Council Heritage Department and Edinburgh Black Cab Tours. Since the Starz production of *Men in Kilts* and my day filming with Graham McTavish and Sam Heughan I have gained a lot of friends from all over the world through Instagram, who all contribute to my little death historian's daily life and as such I would like to thank those two men in kilts and their team. My gratitude also goes to Allyson, Barb, Becky, Bob Proctor, Dave, Fred, Freda, Jan, Jane, Kevan, Lilian, Richard, Robbie, Stephen, Steve, Susan, Tim and William. I have no doubt I've missed out a few names, but as it is currently 4 a.m. I can hopefully be forgiven. A final thanks goes to all those who help preserve the important heritage and history of our precious burial grounds whether physically, through taking photos or recording documentation.